PERE MARQUETTE RIVER

PERE MARQUETTE RIVER

Matthew A. Supinski

A Frank
mato

PORTLAND

River Journal

Volume 2, Number 4, 1994

Since the age of six years, Matt Supinski has chased trout and salmon with a fly rod all over the world. Growing up on the Niagara River and Lake Ontario in upstate New York, he remembers his first experiences with the newly blossoming steelhead and salmon fishery of the early 1970s. He cherishes his years living in Washington, D.C. where he refined his skills on the unforgiving limestone spring creeks of Pennsylvania's Cumberland Valley.

Today he and his wife Laurie live in Grand Rapids, Michigan where he works as a hotel food and beverage director. He states that Michigan is one of the last and greatest frontiers for trout and salmon in the world. He knows of no other place where one can catch Atlantic salmon, 35 pound wild Pacific salmon, 20 pound Skamania steelhead in July and August, and fish to phenomenal mayfly hatches on some of the best trout streams in North America—all in the same week!

Mr. Supinski's writing has appeared in *American Angler, Fly Fisherman,* and other regional publications. His hobbies are photography, reading philosophy and being an incessant connoisseur of food, wine and spirits.

◆

Acknowledgments

Many thanks to my parents and my wife Laurie for putting up with my fanatical enthusiasm. Also to Bob Nicholson of the Baldwin Creek Motel, to Jim, Tom and Chris Johnson of Johnson's Pere Marquette Lodge and to Meryl "Zimmy" Nolph, for their precious time, insight and guidance in helping me understand this great river. To Steve and Charlotte Stallard for streamside companionship and world-class fly tying and to Arden's Photo of Grand Rapids for their quality service and for calling me "Allen."

◆

Series Editor: Frank Amato

Subscriptions:
Softbound: $30.00 for one year (four issues)
$55.00 for two years
Hardbound Limited Editions: $80.00 one year, $150.00 for two years
Frank Amato Publications, Inc. • P.O. Box 82112 • Portland, Oregon 97282 • (503) 653-8108

Design: Joyce Herbst
Photography: Matthew Supinski
Map: Tony Amato
Printed in Hong Kong
Softbound ISBN:1-878175-77-7, Hardbound ISBN:1-878175-78-5
(Hardbound Edition Limited to 500 Copies)

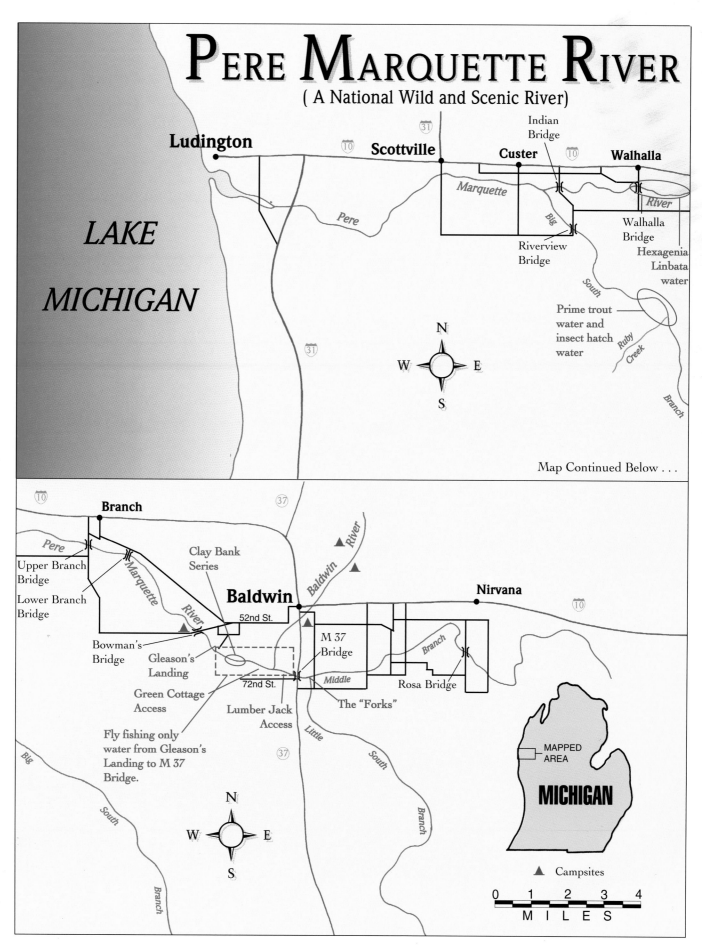

PERE MARQUETTE RIVER
(A National Wild and Scenic River)

Ludington

Scottville

Custer

Walhalla

Indian Bridge

Marquette

Pere

Big

Riverview Bridge

Walhalla Bridge

River

Hexagenia Linbata water

South

Prime trout water and insect hatch water

Ruby Creek

Branch

LAKE

MICHIGAN

N W E S

Map Continued Below . . .

Branch

Pere

Upper Branch Bridge

Lower Branch Bridge

Marquette

Bowman's Bridge

Gleason's Landing

Green Cottage Access

Fly fishing only water from Gleason's Landing to M 37 Bridge.

Clay Bank Series

Baldwin River

Baldwin

52nd St.

River

72nd St.

Lumber Jack Access

M 37 Bridge

Middle

The "Forks"

Nirvana

Branch

Rosa Bridge

Little

South

N W E S

Big

South

Branch

MAPPED AREA

MICHIGAN

▲ Campsites

0 1 2 3 4
M I L E S

Angler casting above the Rainbow Club.

◆

PERE MARQUETTE RIVER

◆

*P*ERHAPS IT IS THE DENSE MORNING FOG OF EARLY May that it starts to happen. The peaty smell of a budding green forest and its marl bogs fills the cold air and stings briskly on your cheeks. That is when the enchantment of this gentle, cool flowing river creeps deep into a fly fisher's spirit.

Winter loosens its grip on this sparse and desolate land slowly. It clings on until spirits are broken—calmed with each intermittent period of sunshine and passing thaw. Spring here is a time of cleansing and promise—renewal ushered in by the scent of fresh pines and undergrowth of ferns, skunk cabbage and wildflowers, freshly sprouted morel mushrooms and the thumping of a male grouse in search of its mate above the Upper Branch Bridge.

As we floated the full, tea-colored river, each bend, pool and riffle revealed the diversity and fertility of this unique river. When the morning sun burned off the last patches of fog and warmed the streambed, we were delighted by a frenzied hatch of golden stoneflies which played reveille on every trout in the stream. It was humorous to say the least—educated trout from last fall's selectivity graduating class missing those aggressively flighted adults—performing a porpoising exhibition that even Seaworld would have envied. Yellow Stimulators, fished grasshopper-style, brought plump browns and rainbows to the net—fish that had recently shared in the plethora of spring hatches and steelhead eggs.

Our eyes were on the prowl for emerging Hendricksons, the hallowed aristocrat of the Catskills. As the waters warmed into the lower 50s, more and more pinkish-gray duns were seen popping to the surface—riding and gliding the gentle currents, struggling to dry their wings in the cold air. The browns were holding in feeding stations tight to the lunker-structure of the clay banks—as if knowing their prey was helplessly doomed to their feeding lane. Concentrating on a deep continuous rise form as opposed to the random dimplings of pre-smolt steelhead, salmon and yearling browns, my Comparadun was refused after several perfect drag-free drifts. Switching to a still-born emerger pattern immediately struck pay-dirt—a feisty 16 inch brown trout worked my drag and the current with an arrogant disdain. *Baetis*, olive stones and *paraleptophlebia* decided to join in the "pleasant time" of the day to create a complex hatch and make things a bit more challenging. We were on a river roll.

After a streamside lunch, filled with imaginative yet somewhat questionable tales by our charming and gregarious river guide, we watched the sun reach the tree-line and then headed for the gravel tailouts in search of the river's princes and princesses—wild steelhead. As predicted we found fresh pods of late spring steelhead—hanging below the gravel—fresh in from the big lake and full of curiosity. An aggressive 10-pound male turned a good distance to slam my *Hex* Wiggle-Nymph with a vengeance, leaping and cart wheeling down the non-stop current. Resilient—that's the best word to describe these stream-bred natives once hooked. You'll hear anglers saying "Hail Marys" as their 4X tippet and tiny nymph hook borders on the verge of destruction. Floating into our take-out at Gleason's Landing we felt complete—after experiencing a truly unique fly fishing river.

I can only use superlatives when speaking of the Pere Marquette. Its cool, spring-fed waters soak up every drop of ground water percolating through bogs and second-growth hardwood forests, creating a smooth flowing river that abounds with life. The current is ever-present yet gentle enough to caress a wading angler or glide a canoeist to his or her destination. Debris: small branches, vegetation and the aquatic biological drift of nymphs and fish eggs, spin and turn against a background of fine glacial sand. Watching the river bottom is very tranquil—nature's hypnotism at work.

To best describe the Pere Marquette I must think back to my native Polish language. This beautiful, yet complex dialect categorizes everything by gender. A Polish demigod of nature must have had insight into the spirit of things during the country's lingual origins to make a river feminine—"rzeka" (gsheka). The Pere Marquette is truly a lady. She opens her gravelly womb to the migrating steelhead and salmon that visit her like prodigal sons and daughters—nurturing their offspring and creating yet another generation of life. She provides haven to resident trout and insects. They rely on her constant water quality, temperature and flows. She gave and gives to all who used and use her—natives, French fur trappers and loggers in an era gone by, wildlife, anglers, canoeists, environmentalists, river guides and hiking naturalists today.

To the fly fisher the Pere Marquette, or P.M. as it is locally known, is a world class trout and salmon river. It can provide the ultimate sporting challenge and enjoyment. Whether you're matching minutiae with delicate size 24 *Tricos* to selective August trout; fishing early summer big bugs like gray drakes and *Hexagenias* to night feeding lunker browns, or chasing wild steelhead and Chinook salmon in the 30 pound range, the Pere Marquette has something for everyone. Many anglers are called to this river each year. But few allow this gentle lady to reveal herself. She gives patiently and selectively to those willing to learn her ways and pay their dues to understand her.

The River of the Black Robe

*I*T IS TO THE WISCONSIN GLACIATION AND OTHER glacial upheavals that occurred over the past 130 million years, that the Pere Marquette watershed speading over 494,000 acres and 762 square miles owes its primordial character and origins. The resulting soil of organic remains and glacial till produced magnificent pine and deciduous forests. The climate was cool and moist, allowing for northern floodplain rain forest to permeate the entire northern and lower peninsula of Michigan.

Due to the sandy soil and bogs holding ground water and precipitation, the river is usually the last to flood its banks due to heavy snow melt or a continuous period of rain. Its tributaries funnel and retain ground water accumulation and act like a chalk stream or spring creek—rarely is the P.M. a mocha cappuccino colored raging beast like other spate rivers. Spring steelheaders, always on the lookout for fishable streams despite miserable conditions, count on the Pere Marquette to be fishable when other rivers are often over their banks.

The watershed was inhabited as early as 10,000 B.C. Paleo Indians wandered north in search of game fish, wild fruit and vegetables. From stone and other minerals, arrows and tools were fashioned to aid in the tribes' hunting activities. The Woodland period (1,000 B.C.) saw the predominant Hopewell cultures practice agriculture on the rich floodplains of the watershed. Conical mounds can still be found in southern Michigan which imprinted this lost culture. Around 1000 A.D.,

Horseshoe Bend at First Claybanks.

Wildflower—fringed polygala gaywing.

◆

the Great Lakes Indian population was dominated by the Ottawa, Ojibwan (Chippewa) and Pottawatomi. Historians have theorized why a proliferation of eastern seaboard based tribes migrated to the Great Lakes. Some say they escaped the European disease flotillas of the French and English—others retreated with the Nordic Viking invasion. The new tribes called themselves Anishnabeg—"first people." These Indians named Lake Michigan after their word for "great water"—Kitchigami.

The French made contact with these tribes after the Vikings. Etienne Brule, in 1662, barred the fruit of a sordid relationship between the whiteman and Ojibwan marked by slavery, corrupt business barter, disease and alcohol. Native cultures were destroyed by their involvement in the French and Indian, Revolutionary and 1812 wars. The U.S. Calvary battle at Custer along the P.M. was the death knell for these river cultures.

In the spirit of manifest destiny, the French government assigned Louis Jolliet to explore the Great Lakes and head waters of the Mississippi. Jesuit missionaries provided spiritual bonding with Indian tribes and established settlements. It was during this westward migration that Father Jacques Marquette joined Jolliet and began to work his magic with the natives. He was a very kind, knowledgeable and charismatic man. His Christian empathy towards the natives and genuine concern over their well-being allowed him to colonize in the name of Christ and "give to Caesar what was Caesar's" (the French king)—new colonies and holdings. Marquette became very fluent in Indian dialects and always knew how to calmly carry himself in hostile areas.

At an amazing pace of 65 kilometers (almost 40 miles per day) Jolliet and Marquette explored the entire upper Mississippi watershed encompassing Wisconsin, Iowa, Illinois, Indiana, Tennessee and finally as far south as the Arkansas River. Deducing that the Mississippi eventually flowed into the Gulf of Mexico, they turned back with the added incentive of knowledge of Spanish armies that were too close for comfort coming up from

the south. In the winter of 1673, Marquette fell ill and wished to return to Sault Saint Marie, a mission that he loved and had established. As the canoe flotilla set out along the eastern shore of Lake Michigan, Marquette's illness became worse and he died ashore at the mouth of the river that bears his name. The Indian natives of this area who were immensely dedicated to him and loved him dearly named the river "The River of the Black Robe," after the Jesuit garment that he wore.

Controlling the region until 1763, the French reaped the harvest of the land and the Indians, sending beaver and furs back to Europe. After the British ceded Michigan to the U.S. as part of the Treaty of Paris after the Revolutionary War, American fur trappers raped the area of beaver—the trees were next.

The building boom of the heavily populated East Coast was underway. Its forests were being cleared at an alarming rate. Michigan was a utopia for pines and other hardwoods. Massive logging began in the mid 1800s. The Pere Marquette river was an ideal target—possessing a good current and plenty of trees along its banks. Decades of massive lumbering left the area destroyed. The banks of the river were pulverized by log jams allowing sediment and other destructive ecological elements to destroy the habitat. As a result of cutting the forest, the P.M. ran warm and murky in the summer. This wanton destruction proved to be too much for the native Michigan grayling which proliferated in this watershed, causing it to become extinct by 1905. With that year being the last log drive, the barren stump-strewn land looked like an atomic bomb had fallen—fires burned, wildlife retreated and man's greed was shamelessly imprinted everywhere.

◆

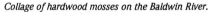

Collage of hardwood mosses on the Baldwin River.

Old Pere Marquette Railroad. Kurt Kale photo.

◆

Aside from the beneficial impact that Jacques Marquette had on the entire area, perhaps no other man influenced the river as indirectly as Fred Mather. As an angler, fish culturist, and U.S. delegate to the 1880 International Fisheries Exposition in Berlin, he met Baron Von Behr, President of the German Fishing Society. After taking Mather to fish for Black Forest brown trout, Mather was amazed by their cunning tenacity and beauty. Von Behr promised to send Mather some eggs. In February of 1883, a batch of eggs arrived in New York where they were divided between the New York State hatcheries at Cold Spring, Caledonia and the U.S. Fish Commission's hatchery at Northville, Michigan. The U.S. Fish Commission, hoping to restore raped watersheds were eager to embark on a new and prosperous era. Newly hatched fry were transported to the Pere Marquette in 1884, thus giving it the honor of the first brown trout stocking in the United States. The fish adapted to the slowly healing watershed and the rest is history.

By the early 1920s, the river had become a haven for corporate Midwest businessmen in pursuit of trout. The Pere Marquette Railroad established access to the river and soon many prestigious fishing clubs emerged, similar to the Catskills. With fishermen came fishing guides who quickly took advantage of the 25 fish creel limits and hammered the river. Yet the bounty of fish increased with the return of the second growth forest. Early P.M. guide boats were about 15 feet long and steered by poles made of ash or maple. Wealthy corporate clients used Garrison bamboo rods and custom tied flies in search of sassy and selective wild browns. The Pere Marquette was back—healthy, beautiful and full of trout.

The Tributaries

*D*EEP GLACIAL SANDS DOMINATE THE ENTIRE geography and nourish every drop of water and assure the P.M. watershed a consistent flow of cool, clear water. Each springtime, when the woods are still barren and the snows have long melted, I revel in driving the backroads near the Little South Branch, Middle Branch and Baldwin Rivers to see springs and tiny rivulets gushing forth next to roadside ditches, people's backyards and flowing from marl swamps and bogs. Watercress and other alkaline loving plants flourish in these springs along with the season's first wildflowers and mushrooms. These tiny veins and capillaries form complex networks that make the P.M. watershed a diverse and great trout and salmon rookery. Fry, fingerlings and smolts abound in nursery waters flowing over fine gravel. The dense forest provides downed trees and stumps (known as sweepers) that harbor excellent native populations of three species of trout. For the small stream fly rodder, the tributaries of the P.M. can take a lifetime to explore. From wet fly fishing for wild brook trout, grasshopper action for plump browns, or battling large migrating steelhead and salmon in close and challenging quarters, the tributaries provide peace and solitude to the exploring angler. Even the locals know surprisingly little about the abundance and diversity that these waters possess.

Each year I learn more about them and retreat to them like when I was a boy exploring brook trout streams in the Allegheny Mountains of New York. Packing a picnic basket, camping, taking an afternoon swim and wildlife watching are very enjoyable along the branches of the river. Catching frogs, watching steelhead fry and getting in touch with nature, can be just as much fun as the fishing. The tributaries allow us to play, forget about time and life's pressure and be boys and girls again. The evolution of an angler begins and ends with things precious and small—seven inch brook trout and 30 pound salmon have their place in that metamorphosis.

The Little South Branch

Newaygo County, named after an Ottawa Indian chief, is a beautiful and undisturbed land first settled by loggers. Dense pines, hardwoods and farm land dot this pastoral countryside. It is in the sunken marl bogs at the Oxford swamp bordered by jackpines and drowned trees that the Little South owes its origin, flowing directly north to meet the main river. A low gradient stream with a silty bottom provides ideal burrowing habitat for gray drake *(Siphlonurus)* mayflies. However, few trout are present in any considerable numbers until the Jackson Bridge area. The Little South is famous for the great Taggert case, involving the U.S. Supreme Court's decision allowing a wading angler to stay in the water even on private property, only to cross at stream obstructions that are unnavigable.

As the creek flows past Jackson Bridge, pool/riffle pocket water develops allowing good native brown trout populations to exist. Deep undercut banks and log jams provide good cover. Many tributary creeks begin to flow into the Little South from here down—all bearing the landowners and farmers names associated with them. Pease Creek and McDuffe Creek provide ideal water for spawning trout and steelhead. I often cannot believe the numbers of spring steelhead that make the journey into these rivulets each spring and provide excellent fishing in a quiet environment. Alders, willows and oaks line this part of the Little South.

From Pease Creek to its junction with the Middle Branch, swift deep pools, riffles and runs averaging 30 feet wide provide excellent trout water with heavy seasonal hatches of Hendricksons, sulphers and caddis. Summer terrestrial fishing to the rare green oak grasshopper can be spectacular during July and August with heavy *Trico* hatches in the mornings. Walnut Road, 17 mile, Forman and the downed Taylor Bridge on James Road all provide angler access points in what is predominantly private property.

The water of the little South is tea-colored due to emanating from marl swamps. Deep dark pools and log jams can hold very big browns. Bait anglers each year pound some trophies out on opening day. Since this is open trout water (bait, spin and fly tackle with a 10 fish daily limit over eight inches) the fish see pressure. Prudent fly fishers time the hatches or fish large black sculpin and Woolly Bugger imitations tight to the banks. You'd be surprised how many 19 inch browns take up year-round residency in this shallow creek.

As the Little South flows past downed Taylor Bridge off James Road and meanders north toward the "Forks," deep pools next to undercut bluffs and long silty runs border private summer homes and cottages. In August the deeper holes can hold some

Turn of the century brown trout stocking train. Kurt Kale photo.

Confluence of Baldwin River on a winter afternoon.

◆

big browns waiting for terrestrials next to the bank—try hoppers, large Stimulators or sculpins in the early morning and evening hours. The Little South ends at Marlborough Bridge on James Road at an area known as the "Forks"—the junction of the Little South and Middle Branch which starts the mainstream of the Pere Marquette. The "Forks" is loaded with gravel at the bridge and the runs below harbor pods of spawning steelhead in the spring. The water is ultra clear and the fish are spooky—use fine tippets and small flies for these aggressive yet selective steelhead. Due to the pool/riffle structure, heavy hatches occur at the forks with excellent populations of wild browns that follow the steelhead migration and tend to stick around all summer because of the cool springs in this area. I have witnessed some of the heaviest Hendrickson, sulpher and *Trico* hatches at the "Forks" with active surface feeding at dusk. Deep pools below the bridge bring out fish you didn't think existed in this stretch.

Little South Access Points

Walnut and 16 Mile Road Access—Take 14 Mile Road east of M-37 for 3 miles, turn left or north on Walnut—cross bridge on Walnut and take a right on 16 Mile Road, go farther north to access Pease Creek area—a Newaygo County map is suggested.

Forman Road Ridge Access Site—Travel south out of Baldwin on M-37 for 3.1 miles to the intersection of Star Lake Road. Turn left (east) and follow Star Lake Road for 3.3 miles to the intersection of Forman Road. Turn right (south) and proceed 2.4 miles to the bridge.

Downed Taylor Bridge Access Site—Lake County—Travel south out of Baldwin on M-37 for 4.1 miles to an unnamed road which goes off to the left (east). Follow this road east 0.5 mile to a north/south road and turn left (north) 0.1 miles to the downed bridge. The Little South Branch in this area averages 30 to 40 feet in width.

The Forks Access Site—Lake County—Travel south out of Baldwin on M-37 for 3.1 miles to the intersection of Star Lake

Road and turn left (east) and proceed on Star Lake Road for 0.4 miles to the bridge over the Little South. Continue 0.1 miles to the intersection of James Road, turn left (north) and proceed 0.2 miles, at which point you will see a large public parking area on your left.

The Middle Branch

Springs gushing forth from the Chase area start the main stem of the Pere Marquette or Middle Branch which flows 17 miles to the "Forks." The bottom is a mix of sand and gravel with ice cold water through summer and good populations of wild brown trout. It averages 15 to 20 feet and has excellent under-cut banks, holes and river bends. It receives little pressure despite the excellent trout population and good concentration of migrating steelhead. This section is a gem to fish if you find the "honey spots."

The upper stretch from Pollaski Road to Nirvana Road is generally 10 to 15 feet wide, brushy and tough to fish with a fly rod—though good numbers of wild browns live underneath hanging tag alders and willows. Once the river reaches the Rosa Bridge area, it widens and provides excellent room for casting. Oak and pine dot the forest and there is little development. The stream here has seen good bank stabilization and lunker structure projects from the 1960s. A tremendous amount of brown trout spawning takes place with often large, holdover winter fish in early spring. Small fly rods 6 to 7 feet are necessary.

This stretch from above Rosa Road to Nelson Road hosts all the complex hatches of the flies-only water. Hendricksons, blue-winged olives, caddis, sulphers, gray drakes and even limited

Wild Pere Marquette steelhead smolt.

Pere Marquette brown trout caught during the olive stonefly hatch.

13

Spawning brook trout.

Hexagenias inhabit this stretch. The native browns in its clear, icy waters can be very selective during hatch periods. The abundance of insects and forms allows the trout to be discerning. *Trico* fishing can also be very reliable during July and August in this stretch.

Perhaps the most famous fishing on the Middle Branch is the excellent hopper activity from mid June through September. A rare green-oak grasshopper inhabits the stretch from Rosa Road to Switzer Bridge, with good bankside grass and vegetation for their propagation. Fish learn early to key on these helpless whirling dervishes of the afternoon. Splattering a lime-green Letort Hopper in the 10-14 size range during a windy afternoon next to the banks can bring up some hefty 14 to 18 inch browns in small quarters. Smaller sizes are advised for early in the season as they grow progressively larger by September. Letort Hoppers are my favorite for these reasons: they float well, skitter nicely and imitate caddis, moths, yellow stoneflies and other opportunistic trout delectables.

As the river winds its way towards the forks downstream from Switzer Bridge, undercut banks, log jams and more stream improvement structures create deep holding water. Fishing sculpins and Woolly Buggers next to these holding areas and stripping them quickly can cause some jarring strikes by big browns— use good size tippets! As the river turns to a more sandy bottom, watch for sand traps that can over-top your waders. Roll casts are often necessary due to the dense over-hanging canopy of trees.

Middle Branch Access Sites

Nirvana Bridge Access Site—Lake County—From Nirvana take Cedar Road south 1.2 miles to the intersection of 56th Street. Turn left (east) and travel 0.4 miles at which point the road turns right (south). You are now on King's Highway and you will continue south 1.8 miles to the bridge.

Rosa Road Bridge Access Site—Lake County—From Nirvana travel 1.2 miles south on King's Highway to the intersection of 56th Street and turn right (west). Proceed 0.5 miles and turn left (south) on Rosa Road. Travel 1.0 mile at which point Rosa Road

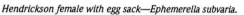

Hendrickson female with egg sack—Ephemerella subvaria.

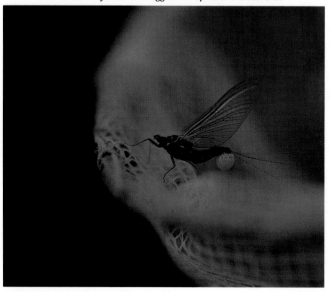

turns right (west) 0.1 mile to the bridge. Good grasshopper stream. Sizeable browns in late summer, spawning steelhead are plentiful in the spring.

Nelson Road Bridge Access Site—Lake County—From Nirvana, travel west on U.S. 10 for 2.5 miles to the intersection of Nelson Road. Turn left (south) and travel 2.2 miles to a dead end where the bridge once existed. Grasshopper fishing for sizeable brown trout in late summer. Steelhead spawn in spring.

Roller Bridge Access Site—Lake County—From Switzer Bridge Access Site, travel south and bear left to the first intersection. Continue and go left at the public access sign.

Switzer Bridge Access Site—Lake County—From Rosa Road Bridge Access Site, travel westward on Rosa Road for 3.0 miles until it dead ends at Broadway, turn right (north) and proceed for 0.2 miles to the bridge.

Thompson's Spring Access Site—Lake County—From Switzer Bridge Access Site travel southwest and then west for 0.9 miles to the end of the good dirt road. Good sized browns in this area—fly casting can be difficult.

The Baldwin River

Cedars, birch and pines line the Baldwin near Luther swamp which provides a spring-fed birth to this important tributary of the main stream. Wild brook trout proliferate in the cold swampy source for several miles until warmer water and lower oxygen levels allow P.M. brown trout to establish their dominance. Cole Creek is an excellent tributary and nursery for brooks, browns and steelhead and is a gem of a small stream for a small rod fisherman using an Adams or hopper. The brookies sparkle with pink and lavender like a Monet and the nearby forest is spectacular in full growth. Below Forman Road, evidence of spring seeps covered by watercress and lime-loving vegetation add water to the river. Deeper holes, undercut banks and log jams hold nice browns— excellent sculpin and Woolly Bugger probing water. Some very big fish come out of these tight spaces each year by bait fishermen. Hatches of *Ephemera,* stoneflies and caddis are present in good numbers with some good *Hexagenia* waters available in the deeper, silty stretches. The state forest campground at Bray Creek offers a beautiful forest setting for the camping angler. When no fish are rising, swing a team of wet flies downstream and across and hold tight for jarring strikes.

East of Baldwin a private trout hatchery sits near the river. Below the rearing ponds an excellent brook and brown trout tributary provides ideal spawning areas for migrating salmonids.

As the river flows near Baldwin, deeper holes hold lunker browns with a respectable *Hexagenia* hatch often bringing these brutes up near 40th Street. The area has dense vegetation and sand traps and is difficult to fish. Ideal cover is present and migrating Chinook salmon frequent this area while looking for gravel. Before entering the main stream, the state public campground is a good area to probe for hatches and migrating salmonids. This area receives very little pressure yet holds some hefty browns.

Baldwin River Access Points

Forman Road/Town Line Bridge Access Site—Lake County— Travel north out of Baldwin on M-37 0.4 miles. Turn right (east) on US-10 and proceed 2.4 miles to Forman Road. Turn left (north)

Gray drake—one of the heaviest hatches on the river.

Turn left (west) 0.8 miles to Sheep Ranch Bridge over the Baldwin River, continue west 0.3 miles to a bridge over Bray Creek and 0.1 miles to the campground entrance on your left.

State Public Access Site—Lake County—Travel west out of Baldwin on 56th Street (Carr's Road) for 0.5 miles to the intersection of Astor Road. Turn left (south) and follow Astor Road 0.9 miles, at which point turn left (east) into the public area.

The Big South Branch

Though often labeled a marginal trout stream, the Big South Branch can produce some of the year's most prolific hatch-matching for lunker browns in the entire P.M. watershed. Mind-boggling hatches of gray drakes, black quills and March browns cover the woods and waters from mid May, bringing up large resident brown trout that inhabit deep, high banked pools and log jams characteristic of this excellent trout stream. Few salmon and steelhead use the Big South due to its warmer water in the fall and lack of spawning gravel when compared to the main stream. However, burrowing *Ephemera* mayflies and fat and sassy browns like the slow, deep tea-colored waters that are difficult to wade and fish.

Originating in Newaygo County at the junction of Winnepsaug and Beaver Creeks, it flows through heavy brush and swamp-laden terrain. These waters support a diverse number of warm water species including pike, bass and a few trout—sucker fishing in spring is the most popular sport on the Big South. Allen and Freeman Creeks join the mainstream as it flows north with Allen Creek producing wild brookies and spawning water in the late fall for browns. Oak and pine uplands along abandoned farm land create strong tea-colored water with seepage from cedar

on Forman Road and follow this road northward 1.9 miles to the bridge.

Bray Creek Access Site—Lake County—Travel north out of Baldwin on M-37 0.4 miles, turn right (east) on US-10 and proceed 2.4 miles to the Forman Road intersection. Take a left (north) and travel 1.0 miles to the intersection of 40th Street.

Fall brook trout in spawning colors.

swamps. This water is tough to read and best fished in evening during a hatch to locate rising fish.

As the stream enters Oceana County, Ruby Creek emits cold water and provides an excellent nursery for spawning browns and hatched fry. Ruby Creek also has large brook trout. Below Ruby there is a chance of catching a trophy male brown just before the season closure. When the hatch is not on ply deep holes and log jams with large streamers—the uglier the better! A 5 pound brown of a lifetime awaits a patient and persistent trophy hunter. As the river flows north to meet the P.M., its waters warm to allow a diversity of warm water fish like pike and bass. The Big South is not easy fishing; it offers lots of exploring for the adventurous. But dividends are often measured in pounds rather than inches.

Big South Access Points

Ruby Creek Public Access Site—Mason County—From Walhalla Road Bridge Access site travel eastward on Hawley Road for 0.7 mile and turn right (south) on Campbell Road. Proceed south for 1.7 miles and turn left (east) on U.S.F.S. 5168 Road. At 1.0 mile, turn right (south) on a dirt road and proceed several hundred yards to the river.

Walhalla Road Bridge Access Site—Mason County—Travel south out of Walhalla 5.6 miles on Walhalla Road to the bridge.

Riverview Bridge Access Site—Mason County—Travel south out of the town of Custer on Custer Road 2.1 miles to Wilson Road. Turn left (east) and proceed 2.0 miles to the bridge. Just beyond the bridge there is state land for parking and access.

The Flies-Only Water—M-37 to Gleason's Landing

As with all great American fly fishing rivers, special regulation stretches attract crowds. When the peak salmon and steelhead runs are on, crowds turn into hoards and then some on this classic water totaling seven miles. Since the establishment of "Flies-only" water, back in the early seventies, "the heart of the P.M.", as many call it, provides the angler with high quality fishing combined with gentle wading or boating waters open year-round. Creel limits call for one salmon or steelhead over 16 inches or one brown trout of the same size during the state's regular season (fourth Saturday in April to September 30th). Fortunately for the avid fly fisher, the crowds are closely associated with short and specific times of the year—the peak of the Chinook salmon and steelhead runs. From about the beginning of September to the second week in October for Chinook and the third week in March to the third week in April for steelhead, this stretch gets "pounded" by yearly pilgrimage makers. But that's only 10 weeks, the rest of the time you will often swear that you were fishing a secret river—that is if you ignore the canoes.

Fly fishing this stretch for brown trout from May to September is perhaps the most rewarding. A diversity of hatches, trout in all sizes and classic riffle-pool-run waters makes trouting an absolute joy and a tranquil experience. Fishing the river during the week or after six p.m. on weekends gives you more privacy from canoeists. Current canoeing good-fellowship codes state that

Michigan salmonfly—giant stonefly—Pteronarcys dorsata.

on national wild and scenic rivers, all canoe rentals obey a 9 a.m. to 6 p.m. put-in and take-out policy. Many horror stories have appeared in the national press lately about "screaming flotillas of drunken fools" ramming their aluminum crafts into the banks, fishermen and anything that stands in their uncontrollable way. You will definitely witness these scenarios. But I have seen a new breed of P.M. canoeist that has values. They behave, are swift, agile and quiet like the Pottawami Indians so as to spot more wildlife, and generally have more respect for the wading fly fisher. Despite all the obstacles to solitude, this stretch of river was created for the visiting angler and P.M. regular. Each year I learn more about it. Classic waters evolve with the seasoning of an angler. As one desires intimacy with this river, the lady of the P.M. reveals and hides on her whims—not necessarily on your terms of yearning and desire.

Starting at the M-37 bridge, the river flows through classic riffle/pool water with good steelhead holding in the pools below the riffles in spring. As the river drifts past Pine Hollow, deep runs in tight under-cut banks hold good browns. *Tricos* and *Ephemerella* hatches are good in this area. The late Larry Westerville's home was here and at this spot early Pere Marquette Watershed Council meetings took place—Jim Johnson, owner of Johnson's Pere Marquette Orvis Lodge, lives on this stretch. The fly fishing is pleasant along this easily wadable stretch, with cabins and summer homes dotting the banks. This area is often overlooked by fishermen seeking the larger waters and drift boat trips below Green Cottage. This stretch offers reminiscences of early anglers trying to provide better habitat and fish cover like old time river guide Simmi Nolph. Campbell's Run, the Dock Hole and the Spring House area all have good holding water and pleasant casting. The bird dog gravestones near the gazebo hold special meaning for river guide Bob Nicholson. Stop by his Baldwin Creek Motel and ask him to elaborate.

As you approach the Flint Rainbow Club property which starts above the railroad trestle, outstanding hatch-matching water is available for selective browns that live in the dark under-cut and log jammed pools—steelhead also favor this stretch. The riffles below the train trestle have excellent hatches of many species if your timing is right. Drift teams of wet flies tight to log sweepers and overhanging cover before the hatch period for some good fish. As the river comes close to the railroad track's stone embankment, deep dark holes hold good fish that come out during heavy gray drake hatches. Some hogs live in this stretch and must be patiently stalked after dark. Steelhead also bed heavily in this section near the club. Under the iron walk bridge at the Rainbow Club, is a good pool and run with a nice gravel tail-out holding opportunistic trout relishing the hatches and gobbling anadromous caviar and fry to stay plump and selective.

As you approach the Lumberjack public access, a good "wading float" of the upper stretch has its take-out here. The entire fly fishing water all the way to First Claybank and slightly beyond is easily wadable during average water conditions—"Wading Float I" takes place between M-37 to the Lumberjack access. Remember—Michigan law allows you to fish through private property as long as you stay in the stream, only to cross property at stream obstructions tightly to the bank until wading is possible again. Landowners have hired off-duty police officers to patrol the banks with walkie talkies.

Below Lumberjack, Mann's Cottage near Cedar Run holds some nice riffle/run water with consistent hatches of *Trico's* and gray drakes in addition to an excellent fishing hole at Chuck Smith's. Each year I hook more steelhead, salmon and early hatch-feeding browns along these stretches than anywhere on the river.

Excellent stonefly hatches bring out some nice browns. A trout, steelhead and salmon angler can spend a whole day in this area. In May, carry a trout rod and steelhead rod as hatches and bedding fish keep you confused and excited as to which way to turn your attention. Pools deepen as you approach the Barnart's—the riffles near Wade Seely's also offer excellent steelhead activity. Good fast riffles for pocket nymphing are located above the Hook-n-Horn with a large deep holding pool below. As you approach the Fin and Feather, Yellow Cottage and Steketee's, deeper pools and runs should turn your attention to bigger brown trout water with larger flies and holding Chinook salmon in September. The deep pools can be swift here and tail-out into log jams and sweepers—battling a large fish here is a real experience—often resulting in a snagged leader. Browns chase big sculpins and Woolly Buggers fished tight to the bank—be persistent and if the fish just follow your down and across offerings, strip your line faster!

The brown cottage near Steketee's was the site of the Outdoor Life T.V. documentary of Jimmy Dean and Lefty Kreh fishing for Chinook. Each year I marvel at the mid to late May steelhead that use these swift and tight riffles just when you thought steelheading was over for another year. These riffles and runs produce excellent Hendrickson and sulpher hatches during the cold rainy days of May, not to mention the excellent *Baetis* and *Trico* hatches. The swift run near Zimmy Nolph's house holds some large browns in the summer that enjoy the deep oxygenated waters—Woolly Buggers fished deep will often turn a nice brown or possibly a summer steelhead.

Another full bodied Pere Marquette brown trout fat from the hatches.

As we near the confluence of the Baldwin River, our "Wade Float II": Lumberjack to the Fisherman's Trail, concludes with the wooden U.S. Forest Service fishermen's steps on the south shore by the streetlight downstream from Doc Green's house. The ledge hole located on the south shore provides excellent holding water for all three migrating species in addition to native browns holding for spent spinners tight to the bank that drift down from the Baldwin. To access, follow the path along the bank and take the trail left (south) at the U.S. Forest Service Stream Improvement sign—this will take you to 72nd Street.

Downstream from the U.S. Forest Service Fisherman's Trail, some of the most popular and productive pools await the angler. The Ole Hole has deep submerged wooded debris that harbors large browns with good gravel stretches below. By Elsie Smith's place sometimes a few summer run steelhead hang out due to the cold spring water ground seeps. As you approach Bawana's Bend and Tom Jack's, you'll find good runs and hatching activity water. The famous Whirlpool Hole attracts salmon anglers in the fall as the Chinook school up and wait to hit the gravel. Below the Whirlpool, excellent *Trico* hatches take place and one can take a salmon rod and a light 2 or 3 weight rod in late August or early September and fish for salmon at dawn and wait for the *Trico* hatch to start around 9:00 a.m.—combination fishing is the beauty of the P.M. at certain times of the year.

Deep bends and swift runs characterize the water as it flows towards the Green Cottage access. This is excellent trout and salmonid water with many underground springs feeding the area.

Hatches abound and steelhead use the deep runs to spawn in spring. Excellent blue-winged olive hatches occur here on June mornings. Fish big ugly Woolly Buggers tight to banks when nothing is going on hatch-wise. This stretch is extremely popular around Bass Wood Run and the Island Hole. Our "Wade Float III" ends here at the Green Cottage down from the U.S. Forest Service Fisherman's Trail.

From the Green Cottage access off Peacock Road and 72nd, beautiful pool/riffle/run water exists with excellent hatches of sulphers, blue-winged olives and gray drakes. Good holding pools exist at the Spruce Hole near the Hearthstone Club waters with excellent deep gravel redds for steelhead at Shopton's Run. Good *Trico* water exists all the way down from the Green Cottage to this area. As we pass the first Burnt Cottage a long stretch of gravel proceeds the Session's water at the First Claybank with intense steelhead and salmon spawning occurring. A deep pool at the bend of the clay banks holds migrating salmonid and some lunker browns that will chase a larger streamer at dusk and dawn.

Below the First Claybank is "The Deer Lick," made famous by an article in *Field & Stream* by Ernest Schweibert. Excellent steelhead redds along with trouty looking water make this area a year-round fly fishing hot spot. The Swing Hole immediately below holds some decent fish often seen on a clear sunny day. At the Second Claybank the Pere Marquette Rod & Gun Club waters begin. Along the clay bank good trout sipping water exists tight to the bank during dense hatches—the fish can be very selective. The Spring Hole below maintains good numbers of holding fall

Brown trout caught on a caddis pupae.

Author's spring steelhead fly box for the Pere Marquette.

stump put in by Zimmy Nolph years back is cable anchored to provide fish cover. The Sturgeon Hole below is marked for some sighted sturgeon seen years ago.

The Jorgenson's land, which is now owned by the U.S. Forest Service, has some excellent trout water which is rather shallow. But good debris and insect hatches congregate feeding browns in the spring. Wet fly fishing or matching the hatch is very productive. A U.S. Forest Service trail leads here from Gleason's Landing for wading fishermen. The High Banks above Gleason's is an excellent bend pool with good rock bank cribbing that holds some very selective browns. Work it hard and wait until the evening hatch for fish to show. As you approach the old Rainroad Bridge trestle, good steelhead spawning water is found upstream. Occasionally *Hexagenia* hatches show in this silted area. Gleason's Landing, marks the downstream portion of the flies-only water.

The Big Water—Gleason's Landing to Walhalla and Beyond

The essence of the Pere Marquette is embodied in the big water of its lower stretches. This Natural Wild and Scenic River truly fits its description here with more federal land, fewer cot-

Author battles a leaping May steelhead above Zimmy Nolph's.

salmon—excellent debris immediately downstream posses good browns but is fishable with surface flies only. At the Third Claybank Hole, huge browns hold against the rock rip-rap ledge when the sulphers are hatching and can be very demanding in the swishing current, deep ledge drop offs make drag-free floats difficult—the pool is definitely worth concentrating on during hatch periods. Immediately below the Third Claybank is a short stretch called the Rapids—a very popular harboring area for spawning and summer run steelhead. Woodpecker Island is a hotspot for guides to park their boats, claim their ground and spot steelhead.

Past the Fourth Claybank, another good holding pool exists for feeding browns, along with the wooded debris and log sweepers of Alligator Alley below. This area is popular for enticing large browns out of the banks, log jams and stumps with ugly black streamers. Old "fish hides" built by longtime river guides Zimmy Nolph and Herman Stephanson are still found here dating back 60 years. Wadel Riffles is an excellent hatching area for mayflies and stoneflies and looks similar to stretches of the Ausable—log sweepers and gentle wadable water. Deep runs hold fish all year below the riffles.

Below Wadel Riffles, Geiser's Bend is the home pool for the P.M. Rod & Gun Club—Danaher Creek enters the mainstream in this area. It is excellent pocket nymphing water for steelhead and browns. The Sand Hole above Duck Island is quite deep and harbors fall steelhead in its comfortable lies shrouded by heavy wooded debris.

Downstream, the Grayling Hole has large browns, and holding salmonids. The north bank is undercut and provides good lunker cover with submerged logs. As you pass the Frog Pond a large bend known as Cooper's Rollaway has good holding water and excellent Hendrickson hatches in the spring. A large tree tages and private holdings and a deep, dark flowing river that embraces many mysteries.

Beginning at Gleason's Landing, the river averages 60 to 85 feet wide with deep swift runs that can be tricky in the high water. The area is popular with steelhead fishermen both in the fall and spring. Sand, gravel and deep wooded debris combine to make good brown trout holding and feeding lies. When drifting or wading the lower water look for "gnarly stumps and old trees" as river guide Bob Nicholson describes them. Despite the fact that some of the water doesn't look like *Ephemerella* hatching areas, excellent Hendrickson and sulpher hatches occur in spring. Due to the slow sandy flat areas, the bugs float helplessly for long periods on cold spring days to trigger feeding activity. When fishing Woolly Buggers and large sculpins strip them using mini-sink tip line on a stout leader over wooded debris and sweepers next to shore—hold your breath as monster browns pursue your offerings passionately—twisting, flashing and just missing most of your presentations. Bob Nicholson's hook up ratio is about one in seven. It's tough fishing—lots of hauling and stripping. But it sure pays off. For many years I refused to "chuck-and-duck"—being a dry fly purist during trout season. I've recently changed my tune and fish lead-head black uglies behind woody debris and undercut banks.

At Bowman's Bridge, a large federal campground and landing signal an excellent float trip through classic trout water. Though the first mile or so of the river is primarily sand and silt, deep pockets near shore hold good brown trout that fall victim to bait fishermen each spring. I'll never forget a spring float near Bowman's when I asked a group of worm anglers on a cold afternoon in a facetious manner, "How'd you do?" Much to my amusement they held up a stringer of what at first looked to be fat carp. But a second take showed fat golden fish with spots!

Hex dun deer hair parachute.

Many underground springs seep in below Bowman which keep the river cool in summer. MacDougal's Lodge is famous for its launching of the old P.M. river boats used by Zimmy Nolph and Herman Stephanson and an excellent fall steelhead run exists tight to its banks. As you approach the Cannon Ranch and Kinney Creek, itself a fine trout tributary, you'll notice casting platforms built in the old days for vacationers to enjoy and overlook the river—some big browns inhabit the deep pools and tight rock

Large male winter steelhead.

Sunset at the dunes of Ludington, the mouth of the Pere Marquette.

structure in this area. A main lodge and four cabins cover a long distance of the Cannon Ranch with lots of stream structure and rehabilitation of the river performed by landowners 50 to 60 years ago. Above a low wooden bridge exists "alligator water—meaning large predaceous fish" as Bob Nicholson describes. Fishing a dark ugly can bring up trophies. When fishing the lower water during the day when there are no hatches, fish attractor dries like the AuSable Skunk, Mattress-Thrasher and Stimulator.

An amazing amount of Chinook and steelhead fry migrate through this area in spring, making for excellent white streamer fishing to cannibalistic browns—tie the flies light and refined. Deep dark pools and sweepers continue to dot the river all the way to Rainbow Rapids which holds good surface feeding trout in the evening tight to the high banks.

From Rainbow Rapids to Lower Branch Bridge, excellent and scenic water exists in a swift and narrow flowing river—alternating high banks are more than 20 feet high. The Sulak Public Access Area allows the walk-in angler a chance to enjoy these prime trout and salmon areas. Good spawning gravel is available through the entire stretch—although this is primarily holding water, with excellent lunker brown trout structure. Usually late in the *Hexagenia* hatch this area produces well as the bugs migrate upstream and find the silt runs to their liking. This stretch holds famous pools such as the A-frame Hole, the Stump Pool, Swimming Hole, Clay Pool, Barnett's Rapids and County Line.

From Lower Branch Bridge to Walhalla is definitely the super lunker brown trout section frequented by *Hexagenia* matching fly fishermen. Lots of high banks with rock rip-rap structure recently provided by the Pere Marquette Restoration Council provide deep water. The big boulders you often see here are clay. A tremendous infusion of underground springs keeps water temperatures cool as evidenced by aquatic vegetation patches. Famous pools like Big Bend, Clay Hole, Slide Pool and Atkinson's Run hold good brown and anadromous fish.

Buck Creek and the Maple Leaf area provide tremendous Chinook salmon spawning especially above the second Burnt Cottage. A U.S. Forest Service access area and stream restoration area is located here. Barothy's Lodge has good spawning gravel and structured riffles excellent for wet-fly fishing for brown trout. The lodge has excellent accommodations for corporate retreat groups and fly fishing groups—in addition to just nice family summer vacations.

Below Barothy's is the famous "*Hex* water." Big browns feed to heavy *Hexagenia* hatches with larger wooded debris sheltering the lunkers. Outstanding *Isonychia* and gray drake hatches blanket the water in May with blizzard hatches. This area is an insect refuge all the way to Walhalla Bridge.

Below Walhalla, the river deepens and contains heavy log jams and mosquito infested dense woods and bogs. *Hex's* by the "billions" ascend from swamps near Indian Bridge and provide blanket spinner falls. Weldon Creek above Indian Bridge is an excellent brown trout and nursery water stream.

At Custer, the area of one of the last Indian Wars, the Big South enters and the river is a vast winding wetland of divergent river courses, swamps and marshlands. Pike, bass and other warm-water game fish are numerous, in addition to the migrating steelhead and salmon in season. The area between Scottville and Ludington is perhaps the most wild and undisturbed wetland in Michigan. Ocean-sized steamers carry cars and passengers to Wisconsin from Pere Marquette Lake at the mouth across Lake Michigan.

Hatches

"One such riffle in the Pere Marquette River in Lake County, sampled in May of 1947, yielded nymphs of thirty-three species."

Mayflies of Michigan Trout Streams
Justin and Fannie Leonard

*T*HE AQUATIC AND TERRESTRIAL INSECT LIFE OF THE Pere Marquette is astonishingly rich and diverse. Perhaps second only to the AuSable River near Grayling in terms of insect numbers and diversity, the P.M. can easily be labeled one of the finest hatch-matching rivers in the country. From its ice-cold tributaries with aquatic vegetation and gravelly riffles it provides ideal habitat for free swimming and clinging mayflies and stoneflies. The main rivers diverse structure of pool, riffle and silt-ridden eddies provide excellent habitat for the above mentioned species in addition to caddis and the large burrowing drakes like the Hexagenia and Siphlonurus.

Though Pere Marquette trout are usually very opportunistic feeders, having to brave bitterly cold winters and the onslaught of migrating salmon and steelhead, the dense hatching period can find them selective about imitation and presentation. There are times during the gray drake and *Isonychia* hatches when there are a ridiculous amount of insects on the water—blanketing every square inch. Recent studies on the river by Indiana University's School of Public and Environmental Affairs show a continued increase in both numbers and species of aquatic insects over the past several years.

Stoneflies *(Plecoptera)* are usually the first insects to emerge right after the new year. Along with mayflies, their life cycles are incomplete: having the stage of egg, nymph and adult—minus the pupae and larval stages of the complete entomological order. Life cycles range from one to three years. Stoneflies are crawlers. They can be agile on stream bottoms but very clumsy swimmers—most often crawling out on rocks, bridges and tree trunks to emerge. During their several moltings they become vulnerable to trout, salmon and steelhead smolts. It is no wonder the stonefly nymph is perhaps the single most deadly fly on the river.

On warm winter days in January and February tiny winter black stoneflies *(Allocapnia* and *Nemouridae)* hatch during sunny afternoon periods. It is often humorous to watch these little black stonefly processions along the snowy banks wandering aimlessly. Good populations are found in the upper stretches of the flies-only water with most fish concentrating on the nymphs since dry fly action is usually not on the trout's agenda with water temperatures in the mid to lower 30s—especially to size 16 to 20 flies.

It is the early black stone *(Taeniopteryx)* that makes it's heaviest impact on the trout and steelhead in March and April. Running size 10 to 12, heavy feeding takes place during the steelhead migrations as their redd digging dislodges substantial numbers of nymphs into the drift along with the crawling emergers. The early brown or olive stone *(Brachyptera)*, medium brown stone *(Perlodidae)*, and little yellow and green stone *(Alloperla)* are intermittently scattered from April through October. They often create complex hatch situations on the P.M. with the scheduled emergence of the various mayflies. One in particular, the early brown or olive stone usually hatches around the same time

Laurie Supinski looks to the sky for the Hex hatch. This scenario presents itself nightly from when the gray drakes start up to the Hex hatch. The water is below Walhalla Bridge.

in the afternoon as the Hendricksons and is very similar in size and color. The Pere Marquette is notorious for complex hatches. Close inspection is required especially with stonefly and caddis hatching.

The giant *Pteronarcys dorsata,* or Midwest salmonfly averaging about size 2 to 6, stir up a lot of feeding commotion when they hatch during evening and early morning hours of May through early July. They tend to favor the swift current of the upper flies-only water and the area near Rainbow Rapids. Impressive browns are caught during this hatch especially by night fishermen stripping large nymphs near the shallows after dark. Though the great majority of stoneflies emerge from the shore or stream structure, the early olive-brown stonefly and little yellow will often emerge from the stream's surface, thus the con-

Hexagenia limbata—Hex.

fusion with other early emerging mayflies. Excellent stonefly water exists from Wadel Riffles near the Fourth Claybank on the flies-only water all the way upriver to the forks. Stimulators in various sizes and colors fished grasshopper style tight to the banks can provide for some explosive dry fly action.

The first mayfly of prominence to emerge in spring is the Hendrickson *(Ephemerella subvaria).* The hatch is very predictable on the P.M. with the afternoon period from noon to three showing the greatest emergence of these pinkish-gray flies from late April through May. Swimming in up-and-down vertical motions, wiggle-nymph patterns excite a lot of browns. Emergers work very well on cold, damp days when the flies struggle to break the surface. Duns floating the surface for long periods of time during inclement weather should be imitated by a comparadun with a long drag-free float. Spinner falls occur around four or five o'clock in the afternoon—later in evenings during warmer, sunnier days. Try to imitate the orange colored egg-sac of the female with sulpher Antron at the tail of your imitation—the Lady Beaverkill Adams is a good choice. Good Hendrickson water exists on the Little and Big South branches and also from Green Cottage to the railroad trestle below M-37 on the flies-only water.

Hatching simultaneously with the Hendricksons are bluewinged olives *(Baetis vagans)* and slate-winged mahoganys *(Paraleptophlebia adoptiva).* The tri-brood *Baetis* nymphs are rather fast swimmers. Imparting action to your Pheasant Tail Nymph, which is a good generic imitation (tied with a peacockherl thorax), will help you get more strikes. Cloudy overcast days with drizzle are excellent hatch periods for the phototropic blue-

Brown drake—Ephemera simulans.

winged olives. The second brood that hatches during middle to late June can provide outstanding rainy morning fishing often overlooked by anglers sleeping-in in order to concentrate their nights on the *Hex* hatch. Similar in appearance and size to the *Baetis,* mahogany nymphs share the *Baetis*'s love of sweeping gravelly riffles with vegetation and debris—congregating and schooling in the side eddies of the P.M. When trout are targeting mahoganys, they can be very selective to delicate, reddish-brown duns.

The marl-bogged and tea-colored Pere Marquette, with its sluggish silted eddies and tributaries produce some of the most amazing black quill *(Leptophlebia cupida)* hatches in the country. The chestnut colored nymphs and blackish -brown duns and spinners with marked bands are very important to the streams of the central, lower peninsula of Michigan. Though the duns are often not visible on the water due to the nymphs preferring to crawl out at emergence, spinner falls can be dense, occurring in early evening hours.

I recall a pleasant late afternoon on the Big South Branch in May when thinking about these flies. Due to the numerous dirt back roads of the U.S. Forest Service near the river, I boldly took

Isonychia—white gloved howdy.

Chartreuse Candy-Cane Woolly Bugger　　　　Peach Candy-Cane Woolly Bugger　　　Egg Sucking Leech
Tiger　　　　　　　　Thugmeister
St. Mary's Spey　　　　　Popsicle
Rainbow Smeltania　　　　Steelhead Sex
P.M. Edgebright　　　Hex Wiggle-Nymph　　　Kaufmann's Black Stone　　　Super Freak Hare's Ear
Green Rock Worm　　　Hare's Ear Rubber Legs　　　Hare's Ear Wet Fly　　　Shrimp　　　Steelhead Mayfly Bead-Eye
Spring's Wiggler (low water)　Spring's Wiggler (cold water)　Apricot Roe-Bug　Oregon Cheese Glo-Bug　Cotton-Candy Glo-Bug　Apricot Supreme Glo-B

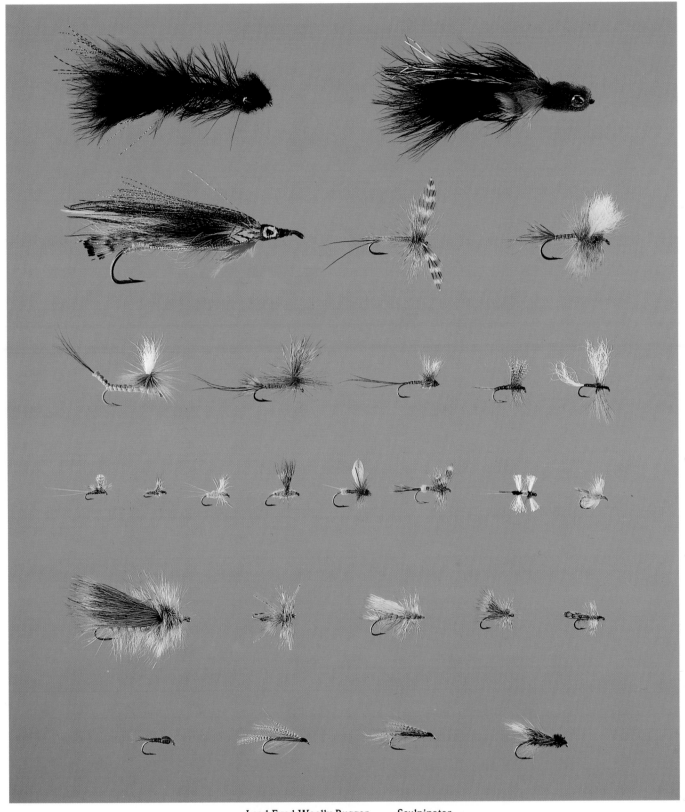

Lead-Eyed Woolly Bugger   Sculpinator
Smolt   Yellow Sally   Trico Double
Lady Beaverkill Adams   Hendrickson Female-Eggsack   Hendrickson Comparadun   Sulpher Compara-dun   Blue-Winged Olive Compara-dun
Mahogany Dun (Paraleptophlebia)   House and Lot   Borchers   Gray Drake Spinner   Brown Drake   Hex Parachute   Hex Wulff   Hex Spinner
Giant Midwestern Salmon Fly   Mattress-Thrasher Stimulator   Olive Caddis/Stone   Early Black Stone
Pheasant Tail Nymph   Orange Queen of Waters   Black Queen of Waters   Pickett Pen

Angler probes a run above the Green Cottage.

◆

my black 79 BMW (I call it the "Field Car," due to its banged up and tattered condition from many fishing adventures—170,000 miles and still going strong!) down a treacherous short-cut and got stuck in a foot deep muddy slide. Desperately pushing while my wife was praying to the gas pedal, hords of black quill spinners descended on my car in the middle of the forest, mating and laying eggs on my roof, trunk and hood. Dark, shiny surfaces attract black quill and gray drake spinners—perhaps resembling the dark, tea-stained color of the rivers. It was an omen of things to come as we finally got to the river only to be greeted by swarming spinners and ravenous fat browns. The Big and Little South branches and the main river down to Walhalla have the heaviest concentration, peaking from mid May to late June.

Perhaps the most spectacular and unique hatch of the Pere Marquette is the emergence of the gray drakes *(Siphlonurus quebencensis, rapidus* and *alternatus)*. Beginning about the third week in May and lasting until mid June, spinners blanket the entire system at dusk, creating black clouds above the riffles. Occasionally this hatch of size 10/12 mayfly is too dense to fish—your imitation only a speck of sand in a descent of falling and mating spinners. Since duns emerge along the shoreline and in swamps and bogs, the spinner fall is the most important stage. Look for larger trout to hold in eddies below riffles—comfortably gulping globs of spent spinners into the late hours of the night. Frequently massive evening swarms occur with no spent spinner fall due to the swarm containing one gender only—thus no mating. The entire P.M. watershed is infused with this species and it occurs with great regularity. Stay out late, head for the riffles and carry a flashlight and heavier tippet material. The best spinner patterns consist of moose hair for the tail, stripped grizzly and dun hackle quills wrapped as the body in gray and white bands, and clipped dun hackle for the spent wings—a delicate and deadly imitation. Double patterns work very well also. In warmer weather spinner falls occur from 4 to 7 a.m. Though the brown drake *(Ephemera simulans)* has a brief but important hatch period near the middle to late June period, it is a tough hatch to catch and not very reliable.

During the gray drake and brown drake hatches of June, *Isonychias* and *stenonemas* are on the water at the same time, creating a complex hatch mess of reddish-brownish gray flies that somehow look alike. I've had floats down on the lower P.M. to Walhalla with late afternoon and evening spinner falls so dense it looked like someone was floating millions of pounds of sawdust down the river. Needless to say the fishing can be degrading—almost downright impossible. Though the sulphers *(Ephemerella dorothea* and lighter *stenonemas)* are pleasant hatches to fish, they tend to be unpredictable from year to year. Memorial Day weekend to the middle of June will see the greatest numbers. The upper flies-only water from the Third Claybank to the railroad bridge below M-37 is your best bet. The upper Baldwin and Little South branches also have respectable and reliable sulpher emergences. Fish the pre-hatch period with a Pheasant Tail Nymph deep down to humping and rolling trout and switch to a yellow-orange compara-dun and other no-hackle dry flies that work well on the gentle flowing, spring-creek style waters of the P.M.

The lower P.M. has excellent, if not unpredictable hatches of the giant Michigan mayfly *Hexagenia limbata*. This fabled hatch that stirs up visions of 10 pound browns slashing at giant patterns in the wee hours of the night is most reliable from Branch down to Walhalla on the lower river. The hatch usually starts around the second week in June and can go well into July. Weather plays an important factor. Hot, dry days often provide the heaviest evening emergence that begins around 10:15 p.m. The initial hatches emerge from the swamps, bogs and lakes in the lower river near Scottville, and work their way upstream. *Hex* hatches are found all the way down to Lake Michigan. As for the patterns every local fly shop and tier has their personal favorite—some like 'em big and bushy—others more sleek and natural. The Baldwin River also has a respectable *Hex* hatch. Be wary of moonlit nights—the fish can be ultra selective in darkness. Turn to lighter tippets and smaller patterns—set the hook lightly on every splashing rise. That *one* out of a hundred floats can be the ticket.

Late summer fishing is a hodgepodge of minutae and terrestrials with reliable nightly caddis hatches. The *Trico* hatch is very heavy on the P.M. and often overlooked by anglers chasing summer steelhead. Reliable hatches of *Pseudocloean anoka* occur from early July to September like the *Trico* and at times can approach super hatch proportions. Terrestrials such as grasshoppers (especially on the Middle Branch and grassy bank open land of the fly water), crickets, ants and beetles are abundant and relished by summer trout. Since the P.M. usually has water temperatures comfortable for daytime trout activity even during the hottest summers, terrestrials are playing a more important role on this classic hatch-matching river.

Although species of caddis hatches and *diptera* are too numerous to mention, the P.M. has excellent populations of green rock worms *(Rhyacophila)*. Though they hatch anytime in May and June, these free-living caddis (non-case building) are frequently digested by spawning and migrating steelhead and salmon during redd building. Bright green in color, these caddis trigger an attractor stimulated take from migrating salmonids due to their preference for chartreuse. A pattern tied on a Mustad curved hook #37140, with larva lace's chartreuse hollow-body material and a peacock herl head can be deadly for both spring and fall

Trillium—state wildflower of Michigan.

steelhead and brown trout. The pattern is particularly effective for worked-over, shy and selective steelhead on light tippets.

When not hatch-matching, P.M. anglers hammer the under-cut banks, log jams and deep pools with "chuck-and-duck" streamers like Woolly Buggers, sculpins, matukas, egg-sucking leeches and any other large uglies that spell food or aggression to lunker brown, salmon or steelhead. Using lead-head patterns or sink-tips, it's important to fish close to bank structure to smack the big ones. The choice is yours on the Pere Marquette. It offers the angler delicate dry fly fishing or "chuck-and-duck" bombardiering. The P.M. allows our fly fishing personality to develop and demands that we know our bugs. She's a tough river for those who take her lightly. Her tea-colored waters flow bitter-sweet—giving and punishing.

Steelhead

NATURAL DYNASTIES RARELY ARE INDUCED. THE story of the wild Pere Marquette steelhead is an exception to the rule. Few would have thought that a small planting of 25,000 McCloud River, California strain fingerlings in 1883 on the Little South Branch would signal the start of a world-class steelhead fishery. But the renaissance of the West Coast steelhead plantings throughout Michigan's Great Lakes between 1880 and 1893 including Klamath and other West Coast strains which fused genetically with each other, found the cool, gravely waters of the P.M. to their liking. The river was poised to create an empire for the migrating rainbow.

By 1914 runs of steelhead were so thick on the Pere Marquette that laws were being considered to allow for spearing or netting. As a result of modern sport fishing technology benefiting charter captains and stream fly fishers, angling pressure and the stress it puts on a watershed have kept the annual run in a state of balance, with both good and bad years running in a cyclical fashion. P.M. steelhead are here to stay. Leo Mrozinski, District Biologist for the Michigan Department of Natural Resources says "the runs are in excellent shape. Good spawning gravel and holding water are found in the entire watershed including the tributaries. With the lack of dams and obstacles to movement, steelhead trickle up every inch of the Pere Marquette system."

I can attest to this great manifest destiny. Each year during the early weeks of May while fly fishing for trout to black quill hatches on the tributaries, I always wish that I had brought along my steelhead rods. Just when I thought that they were finally gone, allowing me to switch gears to the selective hatch matching that I love, another small batch of steelhead infiltrates my private river stretches and makes me lust for that one last steelhead fix for the season.

To know P.M. steelhead is to cherish them. Their personalities tax the fly fisher's description. Acrobatic freight trains when hooked, they turn downstream in a frenzy using the current to their advantage. They are selective and spooky at times, only to be fooled by a size 12 Hare's Ear nymph that an educated brown trout would relish. Insect eaters, aggressive, phantoms of low-light periods—early mornings and late evenings. Elegant—always in perfect form—cherry red-cheeked males and silvery-pink hued females, such are P.M. steelhead.

Red-cheeked male winter steelhead.

◆

Pere Marquette steelhead are not just lake run rainbows as many skeptics refer to them. They come from West Coast steelhead stock, cross-breeding and blending to establish a unique Michigan strain. Once the eggs hatch from the gravel and the fry turn into parr, Pere Marquette steelhead feed aggressively on plankton, midges and every edible source of food. Schooling in concealment next to shore, they imprint on the ways of the river and her currents—nature's classroom in its finest form. After two years of ravenous feeding they smolt usually during high water runoff of May and June and migrate to the big lake, mostly at night. There they spend up to three years wandering a nomadic path that can take them to the far corners of the upper Great Lakes. Smelt, alewife, aquatic and terrestrial insects and sometimes tiny birds fall prey. Insects continue to imprint a strong food

signal even 20 miles from shore. In temperature inversion thermoclines known as "scum lines," upwelling areas occur. Here, flotsom and aquatic foods are trapped in an endless cycle on the surface. Large steelhead summer in these areas and gorge on surface trapped bait fish, aquatic beetles, hornets and various other freshwater insects. Since the decline of the Chinook salmon fishery due to bacterial kidney disease (BKD), charter captains have tapped into this off-shore fishery with a vengeance, often producing amazing limit catches. This may be one reason why steelhead runs during the early 1990s have been declining—the verdict is still pending. "Scum line" activity keeps P.M. steelhead very active to insect food forms, thus their attraction once in the river to a little nymph or streamer is often reflexive.

The fall run signals the start of the stream fishery. Usually hot on the tail of the Chinook salmon run, steelhead start to stage off the piers in Ludington and shoot up the river during fall freshets. Early to mid November often finds the greatest concentration of fish from Scottville to Gleason's Landing, with a few fish holding in deeper pools and runs of the flies-only section. Fall fishing is like panning for gold, it takes a lot of effort and probing of lies for a few precious and scarce fish. Yet in that magic moment when the fly fisher finds that tightly-tucked pocket in an undercut bank or sweeper next to a pool tail-out, and a mint-green silver bullet slams the fly and takes to the air, an adrenaline rush and unparalleled euphoria grips the angler and makes it all worthwhile.

Once the salmon angling hords have left the river, fall steelheading is some of the most pleasant fly fishing a P.M. angler encounters. Often a warm Indian summer day and a beautiful canopy of fall foliage give you privacy on the river while others are pursuing hunting opportunities. Due to optimum water temperatures in the 50s, steelhead are active and curious, behaving like stream trout. They show interest in insects and bait fish. (Once I caught a fall steelhead whose mouth had two small frogs in it!) Unpredictable fall Michigan weather can make the Pere Marquette hot one day and stone-cold the next. In any case fall steelheading is a gamble. If river levels are low due to lack of precipitation, there might not be a fall run period!

Understanding fall steelhead behavior is half the puzzle to catching them. Why some fish run in fall and the remainder run in spring is a combination of water levels, temperature and genetics. Due to the mixing of West Coast steelhead strains in the early Great Lakes stocking stages, fish from the Shasta, McCloud, Klamath, Willamette and Rogue Rivers were used. Various genetic signals on when to run a particular watershed fused together to make the runs spread from October to May. Studies of the Little Manistee River show that up to 60 percent of the spring spawning population is in the river and estuaries prior to the onset of winter. These figures are often confusing due to the lack of angler success on fall runs. What the fly fisher fails to realize, especially on the P.M., is that spring tactics of heavy split-shot and leaders coupled with gaudier fly patterns often necessary for spring run-off conditions don't work in the low crystal-clear waters of fall. Fresh-run fish are very skittish, especially with the sunlight conditions encountered in late fall. They are not as aggressive as spring fish that have a short time to seek gravel and spawn. Coercing a fall steelhead to strike often involves using tiny nymph patterns size 12 and 14 (wide-gape and heavy forged shank to hold the fish) and long delicate leaders down to 4 and 5X. Fluorescent colors spook fish. If you're fishing tiny Glo Bugs, stick to the duller shades of cotton-candy and apricot supreme.

With the strong urge to spawn not yet so firmly imprinted as it is in spring-run fish, fall runners seem to look for a reminiscence of life in the big lake. Porpoising on the surface at dusk and dawn, holding and marking territorial locations and dominance by males chasing each other relays the communal schooling behavior they are used to in open water. Occasionally I've watched steelhead poke their nose at twigs on the surface. Usually a rise or splash in one pool signals similar activity in pools up or downstream. This exposition of territorial marking behavior makes the fish very aggressive. Using Spey fly patterns incorporating bait fish motifs using Flashabou and marabou in electric blue, pinkish-silver and black and purple combinations provokes violent takes near the surface.

Though fall steelhead often position in the security and comfort of deep runs and holes, on the P.M., they also prefer shallows, sometimes directly below salmon spawning redds to feed on dislodged eggs or nymphs stirred up by late spawners. Also, since they roam the lake's surface with regularity, their top-water preference is projected to river lies given desirable water temperatures.

Divergent behavioral patterns of fall fish from aggressive territorialism to complacent holding, shyness and selectivity dictates two fly fishing presentations. Attractor Spey patterns stimulate and agitate. Small nymphs and tiny egg patterns stimulate the feeding drive insignificant as it may be.

Eighty percent of all my fall steelhead are caught in a classic fall primary lie. The lie is a pool tail-out with a deep pocket either in the middle of the run or tight against the bank with overhanging trees, a log jam, undercut banks or some other sort of obstruction. Such a lie offers steelhead protection and security, comfort from the current and access to salmon redds with the option of both shallow and deep water. Look for these places and fish them hard. During the day fish will hold beneath trees or in the deeper pool. At dawn or dusk they come out and may do their daily ritu-

Pleasant winter angling for steelhead on a sunny afternoon.

31

alistic display. Resting the pool occasionally is a good choice, since fall steelhead are ultra shy.

What we learned last fall about the steelhead's color preferences was revealing. Steve Stallard, an excellent steelheader, fly-tier and stream companion, developed attractor Spey flies made of electric blue, black, purple and silver materials. They were dynamite during the dusk territorial marking patterns. His Thugmeister Speys may trigger enthusiastic responses for different reasons. Our first theory lies in the novelty of their presentation. Hords of bait-casters bombard skittish fall steelhead with fluorescent spawn bags. The novelty of presenting offerings in colors and silhouettes that the fish have not seen repeatedly might account for the strong interest. Our second theory lies in the ability of these patterns to imitate alewives, chubs and other lake-dwelling forage. Until river migration these prey were mainstays of the steelhead's diet as well as daily lifestyle. Also, as salmon runs have declined on many rivers over recent years, the importance of fluorescent colors has taken a major downturn.

When fall steelhead are lethargic or in a holding mood, smaller and more realistic offerings like nuclear roe-bugs, stonefly, or caddis and Hare's Ear nymphs will entice somewhat indifferent fish. This can be a time when repetitive casting to the point of frustration might be what it takes to provoke a strike. Usually, the strikes are gentle—barely a stop in your line bouncing on bottom. Intuition and a sixth sense play a role in hooking steelhead. If you ask a steelheader why he or she set the hook on a fish, most probably won't give you a concrete answer. They might say, "It just felt right."

Fishing primary lies with a two-fly rig allows you to probe the water—and the steelhead's mind—more thoroughly. A chartreuse-green rockworm nymph with a black stonefly combination is one of the more effective nymph rigs. Often the chartreuse nymph will entice the steelhead, but it takes the more natural, less threatening black stonefly. If water temperatures are in the upper 50s, be prepared for an aerial display. Fall steelhead are powerful and will twist and turn on your line with mighty tail slaps. Many times the steelhead will shake the hook only to have the second fly snag it in the fins or tail during the tumbling battle. You could have sworn you saw the fly in the fish's mouth as it leaped, but when you land it, you realize it's snagged in the fin. This is a common occurrence with two-fly rigs.

Here are some steelhead fighting words of advice—keep the fish on a taut line. Keep excess line off the water and let your drag do the work. On two-fly rigs, the dangling fly can snag bottom while playing a fish, so keep your steelie near the surface as much as possible, where it can fight the current. Because of the optimum water temperature of fall, steelhead will be full of energy, so be prepared for long battles. Avoid sudden movements that startle a soon-to-be-landed fish and cause it to surge and snap a delicate tippet.

The bottom line for fall steelheading? When fish are few and far between, stay on the move and look for primary lies. Explore new fly patterns and meticulously fish each lie and run; it can be painfully boring, but you'll connect eventually. Show the fish something different. When fishing in teams, one should use a two-fly rig, while the other uses attractor Speys. Persistence, patience and a great deal of optimism and open-mindedness are cardinal rules for the Pere Marquette steelheader, especially when enduring weather extremes. Practice CPR (Catch-Photograph-Release): Nothing is more satisfying than knowing that the fall steelhead that you released safely will be waiting for your fly in the spring. A steelhead is much too precious to be enjoyed only once.

Due to harsh Michigan winters, the December to February period on the P.M. is quite unpredictable. Occasionally a mild winter will allow for freshets of snow melt and send silver fish upriver when the water hits 40 degrees. Mild winters combined with adequate precipitation can actually provide exceptional steel-

Female steelhead fanning gravel while being courted by a large, dark shadowy male escort.

Hex wiggle nymph.

◆

staging and schooling off Ludington. Falling barometric pressure, a warm spring rain and a slightly milky hue to the river will send steelhead up in droves. Once the water temperature hits the low 40s, you'll find spring steelhead digging redds and fast and frenzied action.

Pere Marquette steelheaders sight fish to fish actively making redds or fish the pockets and runs near stream cover above and below the gravel. The flies-only water is classic gravel riffle/pool/run water ideally suited to the fly fisher. Many challenges which take time to master, face the spring steelheader on the P.M. and each issue is crucial for the steelheaders success.

Spotting fish is an art form. An angler must possess a sixth sense which improves over time and is learned. Due to the tea-colored dark shadowy water of the P.M., combined with the P.M. steelhead's preference for deep pocket gravel, locating fish is even further complicated. Good polarized glasses and a large or long brimmed hat are essential. Treat all long dark shadows as fish until you are absolutely sure they aren't. Fish will often move onto or dart out of gravel beds quickly, so give each area a lot of attention before you move on to another location. Perhaps the most singular difficulty in making a fly presentation to spring P.M. steelhead is judging the depth and velocity of water they are in. In order not to spook fish an angler must stay at a reasonable distance. With shadows and light bouncing off tea-colored water fish appearing to be in only a foot or less water may actually be down three to four feet, that's not including holding in the hollowed-out redd. Having enough weight or mending your line adequately to sweep the fly in front of them at a speed less than that of the current is the trick. Using running lines with weight or a swing swivel is excellent for deep pocket water. Dai-Ricki's shooting line is a great addition to this technique, allowing the fisherman to get a fly line feel with the quick penetration and delicate feel of monofilament. In shallower pockets and runs use dark colored floating lines and a long leader (Orvis's dark gray stealth line developed for New Zealand's clear waters is ideal). It is very important that fish do not get a glimpse of your line or split-shot—they'll spook in a heartbeat. Although it's easier to spot fish with the sun at your back, watch out for your shadow.

heading. Tactics are very refined since the fish are lethargic and the water is ultra clear and low. Anglers usually fish tiny Hare's Ear nymphs (sizes 10-14) on very long leaders with tippets down to 4 and 5X. Walt Grau, long-time Pere Marquette guide, uses Spey rods with strike indicators, allowing the nymph or streamer to slowly probe deep pockets and pools. Anglers using the long leader method often position directly upstream form the run or pool to be fished, using a running line and split-shot or slinky-drifter. The fly is then allowed to sway and spin almost stationary in front of holding fish, giving them plenty of time to make up their mind whether to strike or not. It's almost like stationary bait-fishing—only with a fly. The strikes are very subtle as the fish gently mouth the fly.

Persistence and good boot insulation are the keys for winter steelhead on the P.M. Your thermometer can be your most valuable tool since the P.M. has many spring-seeps throughout its watershed. (Often you'll find holding lies directly below them with upper 30°s to lower 40 degree F. water temperatures.) Check out topological charts thoroughly—you might find some "honey holes" thanks to the U.S. Geological Survey.

The spring run is the motherlode of the Pere Marquette. Peak runs occur as early as the first week of March during milder winters to as late as the last week in April and can wax and wane until the third week in May—provided stream temperatures remain low and adequate water levels are maintained. If one had to pick the most reliable period, the first two weeks of April is best. Weather, however, plays a key factor on the Pere Marquette—more than any other river I've fished. Great Lakes spring steelhead are predominantly driven by water temperature, level of flow, clarity and atmospheric pressure. Ice on Lake Michigan or the lack thereof also determines the onset of the runs

Jack-male steelhead.

Fresh run steelhead on a Glo-bug.

Low-light periods far out produce any other time of day for the steelheader except during winter when the sun's rays might raise a frigid river to desirable water temperatures for steelhead activity. Early dawn, cloudy days and evening are the time to look for P.M. steelhead. "The freaks come out at dark" is the saying on the P.M. When a fishless run during the day explodes with activity in the evening—fish seem to come from nowhere. Since glare is greatly reduced and fish are less shy, sight fishing is ideal. The aggressive competitive nature of courting males will often elicit jarring strikes from otherwise indifferent fish. A female digging a redd often creates a frenzy among courting males—consecutive hook-ups come fast and furious.

Selectivity and fly preference are important when pursuing spring steelhead. When water is on the rise, anglers can get away with larger tippets and fly sizes. But the P.M. normally runs stable and clear. Ultra shy and selective steelhead are a P.M. hallmark. After years of record keeping on fly selectivity, one can usually predict spring steelhead preferences. Fresh-run females when pursuing redds are usually very difficult to coax to strike. An ultra tiny egg pattern in a duller shade of cotton-candy, apricot supreme or Oregon cheese should be your first choice. If the fish has been digging for a few days, a chartreuse green rockworm is effective

Steve Stallard with large male steelhead.

and almost always takes that impossible fish. Digging definitely dislodges caddis and mayfly nymphs with the green *Rhyacophila* caddis being numerous on the P.M. Regardless of how persistent a digging fish is it cannot help but relish these offerings. Male fish show a stronger liking for more realistic and natural nymphal patterns like the *Hexagenia* wiggle-nymph and Hare's Ear. An afternoon hatch of black stoneflies will also catch their attention and stimulate nymph feeding. Males tend to strike nymphs better during the holding phase as opposed to the nest building frenzy. Large egg-sucking leeches, candy-cane Woolly Buggers and anything large, ugly and black will often provoke lashing strikes during the male jousting period—sometimes the bigger the pattern the better. Small yearling browns and steelhead smolts will often try to get in on the mating action only to be chased and nipped by an aggressive male. Walt Grau's Tiger pattern in larger sizes works well in these conditions.

Remember to stalk your areas or runs carefully, waiting until the crowd leaves. Regardless of what people tell you, drift boats spook skittish P.M. steelhead. If you're planning on fishing a known holding area, anchor or dock your boat on the bank well upstream and wade down carefully. Spend lots of time waiting and observing until the fish show. Once they do, give them a chance to settle in before casting.

Though still in the experimental phase, summer Skamania steelhead stockings have adapted well to the Pere Marquette. July and August are the best times to pursue these silver bullets which are unquestionably one of the finest fighting freshwater game fish on the fly rod. Often trout anglers fishing the river with large hopper patterns in summer explode into a fresh steelhead when they least expect it. Experienced river guides who know the coldest runs and holding water can often hook you up with a fish or two from July on.

No chapter on Pere Marquette steelheading would ethically be complete without discussion of sporting etiquette. Since the river has drawn lots of attention in the last few years from drift boat guides, out-of-state fishermen and the press, the flies-only water can be a zoo—a gauntlet of steelhead frenzied anglers looking for the fish of a lifetime. Each year there are stories of guide fights over gravel areas, snagging with large fluorescent flies and overall hoodlum behavior. Big fish sometimes bring out the ugly side in nice angling citizens. When you come to the P.M., relax—chill-out! You are there to enjoy yourself, not fight a turf battle. There are more than enough fish for everyone and they normally reward those who are patient enough to stay out of the bank rush hour and drift boat flotilla. Sixty-six miles of main river and tributaries hold steelhead with perhaps 25 percent of it heavily fished. Bob Nicholson, President of the Pere Marquette Watershed Council, longtime river guide and Baldwin personality extraordinaire told me "90 percent of the fishermen that come to the P.M. think the river starts at M-37 and ends at Gleason's Landing." That statement cannot be more true. I've found fresh steelhead as late as the third week in May on the tributaries of the Little South, Middle Branch and Baldwin River—experiencing total solitude and cooperative fish. Explore the river, don't follow the bandwagon and the P.M. will reward you.

Practicing gentlemanly and ladylike angling behavior is contagious. Don't trespass—stay in the water or within the mean high water mark—Michigan law protects you. Give an angler his or her space. When drifting go around an angler's backside not to disturb the run. Present your fly offering above and swept in front of the fish so as not to "line" or snag fish. Report violators to con-

A perfect specimen straight from Lake Michigan—a female spring steelhead in excellent condition.

servation officers. Lead by example and the runs will be more enjoyable for all.

On a final note, when wading be careful not to walk on tail-out gravel below or in a spawning redd—you can crush and smother thousands of eggs and eliminate unique wild genetic stock. Practice catch-and-release. Avoid fishing to actively spawning females—hooking one can abort thousands of eggs. Revive your fish carefully. Pere Marquette fish need special care and awareness. Every smolt that makes it back from the big lake is a silent victory in the harsh and unforgiving world of the wild.

Wild Chinook

IT IS A FALL EVENING AT A PLACE ON THE PERE Marquette known as Maple Leaf. The leaves are flame orange, the breeze warm, the river teeming with wild Chinook. As I wade carefully into position a large male moves in on the pod of salmon I've been eyeing. This fish seems more agitated, more excited than the others—and it's gargantuan. After three drifts of my chartreuse-and-black candy cane fly, the fish turns quickly and pounds it. For the next 45 minutes, the athletic 30-pounder tests my endurance with its determination. The wild king twists and turns in powerful surges, its wide otter-sized tail slapping my line almost as if to dislodge the hook. With adrenaline keeping me focused, I ignore the cramping in my arms. Finally, I maneuver my foe closer as it tires, and a nearby angler from Kentucky grabs my net and camera. But in the blink of an eye the hook pops out of the Chinook's snout; the hook has straightened and now looks like a crooked needle. The Chinook was too much for the small hook to handle. "What a shame," the Kentuckian says.

Last fall while wading the P.M. with its grand display of radiant fall foliage as my backdrop, I hooked 10 to 15 Chinook, some over 20 pounds, each day. Landing them was another matter. Fresh in the river, they aggressively took my flies and provided me with crashing leaps and freight-train runs, pummeling my shoulders, back and knees. These fish had the tenacity and muscle of a fresh Atlantic salmon or steelhead. As far as this fly angler is concerned, Michigan never had it so good. Wild Chinook are here to stay on the P.M.

Wild Pere Marquette Chinook salmon fingerling caught during Trico hatch.

◆

In an attempt to revitalize the Great Lakes that were decimated in the early to mid 1900s by the Atlantic invasion of sea lampreys which preyed on native lake trout stocks and to diminish alewives that overpopulated and rotted on the beaches, the Michigan DNR had a vision—plant Pacific salmon. Ruby Creek, a tributary to the Big South Branch of the Pere Marquette, was heavily planted with Chinook and coho salmon between 1964-68. The more aggressive and territorial dominant Chinook took hold. Healthy wild strains of Chinook salmon spread themselves throughout the veins of the P.M. watershed like wildfire, relishing the abundance of gravel for redds and lack of stream obstructions. Soon anglers flocked from around the world to partake of the fall ceremonial homage to this noble and gargantuan "king." Tackle shops, guide services, motels and restaurants popped up in Baldwin. The "Boom" days were here.

Unlike hatchery Chinook that are fed pellets in protective runways, wild Chinook, from the moment they hatch, must fend for themselves and dodge predators like kingfishers, osprey, muskrats, raccoons and yearling trout. They learn quickly to conceal themselves and feed aggressively on algae, plankton and smaller insects. I first saw the tremendous capacity for wild reproduction during the spring of 1992 on the P.M. Although the day was bright and sunny, raindrops appeared to be falling on certain sections of the river, the result of thousands of Chinook fry dimpling the surface while feeding on midges and other aquatic insects. While wading the river in the spring for steelhead and trout, anglers witness dense schools of Chinook fry next to shore. The young fish scurry for cover and grab tiny morsels coming their way.

As Chinook grow to smolt size, insects play a major role in their dietary requirements. Then, when the predators reach the big lake, alewives and chubs become their daily fare. Once back in the rivers to spawn—even though a Chinook stops feeding prior to entering the spawning rivers while its stomach shrinks (both males and females) to make room for sexual organs—the salmon's natal memory is triggered by stonefly nymphs and other insects. They elicit a sudden and instinctive feeding response that is not out of nutritional need.

A fly angler who understands the behavior of wild Chinook and is equipped with the right fly patterns and tackle will have an exceptional sporting experience with these valiant and eager game fish.

Triggered by the diminishing length of daylight, position of the sun and water temperature changes, Chinook begin staging near their natal rivers in about mid August. Shortly after Labor Day, massive upstream migrations begin. Cooler nights and a good rain that raises the water level help hasten the run. If conditions are not ideal, salmon will stack in tidal pools, often porpoising in pods. Large streamers imitating bait fish and fluorescent-colored flies work well at this stage, stimulating an aggressive sexual response or sometimes a latent hunger pang. Once the fish move upstream, they waste no time looking for spawning gravel.

Look for bleached-out gravel in riffles and runs above and below pools, especially near log-lined banks. Salmon head to deeper areas and obstructions for cover when spooked or to avoid the sun's rays—a Chinook's eyes are very light sensitive. Gravel areas at tail-outs of pools also will hold salmon—better yet when combined with logs and trees. Salmon and steelhead have an uncanny ability to dig spawning redds in a steady yet gentle flow in the mainstream of rivers, ensuring that plenty of oxygen reaches their eggs. As a result, drought, freeze and shoreline predators have little impact on hatching fry.

Once you've located a pod of spawning salmon the game begins. Most often several ripe hens and dominant large males will be visible, along with a trailing yet enthusiastic group of juvenile jacks—males looking for sexual action or eggs to gobble. Be stealthy: sudden movements and sloppy wading can put fish under cover quickly. Wild Chinook spook easily and won't hit when startled.

The Chinook's color preferences range from black, chartreuse and fire-orange to hints of yellow, silver and purple. The most dependable fly pattern for wild Chinook is probably Kaufmann's Black Stone, since Michigan rivers are loaded with *Pteronarcys* nymphs, on which salmon feed heavily while smolts. Also, the tail-digging of gravel beds dislodges stonefly nymphs and sends them floating, the temptation being too much to resist.

When spawning begins fish key in quickly on drifting eggs.

◆

Fall Chinook that fell for a Thugmeister.

Paired up spawning steelhead.

◆

Yarn flies and Glo-Bugs in Alaskan roe, chartreuse, egg and Oregon cheese colors can be excellent. Tie and fish Glo-Bugs in tiny sizes, for large ones spook wild fish in the low, clear waters of autumn. A popular technique is to fish two flies: an egg pattern on top and a black stonefly on bottom with a two-fly, slip-sinker rig. This allows you to show several options to the fish and let them establish their preference.

When salmon are in a very aggressive mood—fish moving in and out of spawning redds or males chasing each other while jockeying for position and hierarchy—a Spey-style attractor fly or a big Black Woolly Bugger at times prompts jolting strikes. On other occasions, the same salmon will gently mouth or nudge the fly to the side with its nose or cheek. Be prepared for gentle takes as well as rod-pounders. Edge-Bright Speys and a chartreuse candy-cane with black rubber legs are wise choices for this agitation-style fishing, which involves sweeping the fly on a down-and-across drift in front of the fish's mouth.

Still, presenting flies to salmon on the run can be a frustrating experience. There are times when you must make several hundred casts to trigger a strike. Sometimes, though, the fish won't respond. But patience and persistence are the key. There are magic moments, usually around dusk, when the fish become frenzied and hit everything you throw. These rare times create a fly fisher's Nirvana. In the evening, once the sun goes off the water, Chinook come out of their holding areas and become restless. Competitive males are likely takers. Yet even in afternoon a pod of fish in a deep run apparently waiting out the sun and getting nervous about the spawning frolic of the evening, sometimes will pop every stonefly that comes down the pike. The bottom line is this: You'll never be able to predict the mood of a wild salmon.

Approach wild Chinook as you would wary trout. Change fly sizes, tippet diameters, amount of split shot, lines, etc., until you've found the magic touch. Often, migrating Chinook roll on the surface in an act that appears to mimic a trout rising to surface insects. But they are not surface feeding. This is a way that migrating salmonids, which are used to the varying depths and water pressures of the open-water lifestyle, adjust their air bladders and equilibrium in shallow water.

When fishing a spawning pod, please refrain from fishing to actively spawning pairs. Concentrate on fish in the perimeters, especially aggressive males or females that have not quite found the right spot for their redd. If you wish to keep salmon for the table, take the males and gently release females without dislodging their precious cargo. One dominant male often will mate with several females, so milt is not in short supply. If you accidentally foul-hook a salmon, break it off as soon as possible because you'll have a tough time landing this very powerful fish. Otherwise, you might damage your equipment and exhaust the fish to death—not to mention yourself.

With a little practice in presenting your flies, learning to spot holding and spawning lies, and a good pair of polarized sunglasses, you'll be well on your way to fighting wild Chinook on a fly rod.

Providing you have the right tackle, line and physical endurance, battling a 25 pound wild, fresh-run king on a fly rod can be an exhilarating experience. Once a fish is hooked, don't let it make too many moves or you'll be sorry. A fish heading for a stump or a downstream set of rapids also can spell trouble. Be firm, push your tackle to its limits and take risks. When a fish runs, use your drag and let it ride. Then try to regain lost line once the salmon settles. Stay mobile, follow your fish and be pre-

Author with wild Chinook caught on Hex wiggle nymph.

◆

pared for a downstream decathlon. Last fall I landed a fresh-run, 35-pound female on a size 10 Alaskan roe-bug after an hour-and-50-minute battle that ended about 150 yards downstream.

If possible, try to get downstream of the fish, allowing it to fight you and the current. This tends to tire the fish more quickly. Because of the dense bone and cartilage of a spawning Chinook's mouth, use barbed, laser-sharpened hooks. Be sure to carry a hook sharpening file, too. And when a leaping salmon sprints downstream, take pressure off the line in anticipation of a leap; otherwise, it will shake the hook effortlessly.

Remember to tame and discipline your fish. A brisk fight and a quick landing is a winning situation. Use a good net because hand-tailing results in too many break-offs. Nothing is more disheartening than watching a Chinook swim away with your fly in its mouth after an hour-long battle.

So be humble, be prepared, have your hooks sharpened and wait for the fish to be in the mood. Besides, what could be better than enjoying an Indian summer day, sitting and watching the wildlife before winter sets in. Perhaps this is why fly fishing is known as the quiet sport. That is, until you do battle with a wild Chinook.

Nine- and 10-weight graphite rods with fighting butt sections are the rule. Sage's RPL-X graphites and Orvis' Power-Matrix series are the best I've tried. Orvis' DXR direct-drive and anti-reverse reels can't be beat for price, value and endurance. Floating fly lines in shallow water and Teeny nymph lines are necessary in deeper runs and pools. In addition, make sure you have at least 200 yards of 30-pound backing. Stout 0X to 1X tippets, ranging between 14 and 16-pound test, are strongly advised. On a long downstream fight, a wading staff can come in handy.

Ethics and honesty are necessary when trying to hook salmon. Many overzealous drift boat guides looking to satisfy clients and put them on fish and film quickly, have developed a technique called "lining the fish." When fishing two-fly rigs, some unreputable guides will yell to the client to set the hook after spotting the flies near the salmon, regardless of whether a fish showed interest in the flies. Yet there is a misconception surrounding snagged fish: Some guides tell clients the fish jump only if hooked in the mouth. Contrary to popular opinion, snagged fish will leap. And unethical captains hoping to get a springing Chinook on film will foul-hook fish intentionally.

Snagging fish has other ethical—and legal—implications. The only way you can tell if a salmon is hooked legally (in the mouth) is by watching its head movements. If it wags its head from left to right like a dog's tail, chances are the fish has something in there that's bothering it and it is indeed hooked legally.

Laws legalizing snagging were a big mistake. In 1993, The Big Manistee (Manistee County) and Pere Marquette (Mason County) were the last areas to allow snagging. After October 25th of that year, snagging was a thing of the past. Unfortunately, some snaggers infiltrate the "fly-fishing only" section of the Pere Marquette River with a deceptive snagging device known as the "Manistee Dry Fly." The rig uses a small treble hook with weight and an attached piece of white marabou or fluorescent streamer hair as a sight-fishing indicator. The snagger drops the rig in front of a spawning salmon and tries to hook the salmon near the head, using the tied indicator as a spotter. To report snaggers, look for a local conservation officer or call DNR game enforcement officials at 1(800) 292-7800 for more information or to find the names of conservation officers in the area you're fishing.

As catch-and-release fishing continues to grow, water quality

Doe along the lower Pere Marquette.

◆

and habitat improvements are made and snagging becomes a thing of the past, Michigan's wild Chinook salmon are on the verge of a new and prosperous era.

Although bacterial kidney disease (BKD) has ravaged Chinooks in hatcheries, wild Chinook are less stressed and therefore less susceptible to catching the malady.

Chinook usually congregate and stage in Lake Michigan off the Pere Marquette at Ludington about the middle of August—shooting up the river in schools after darkness falls. Pods of fish usually hold in the deeper pools and channels near Custer and Scottville around Labor Day waiting for colder nights and fall rains to shoot them up the river. Nearly every gravel bed from Walhalla to the upper tributaries will hold good pods of spawning fish, with the flies-only area from Gleason's Landing to M-37 and the Baldwin River having excellent numbers and aggressive fish. The Big South, initial nursery water, has good runs of Chinook still strongly keyed to their mother stream.

A word of caution. When salmon are in, the river is a madhouse of crazed anglers looking for their trophy of a lifetime. Don't get caught up in the insanity. Fish the river in the evening or during the week. Wait until the flotilla of drift boats and wanna-be guides have spooked or foul hooked these beautiful fish into hibernation and retreat. There's no hurry. More than enough fish for you and your companion's fly rods to handle are available. When guides are towing their boats out of the landing, make the "quiet time" to your advantage. The fish sense the frenzy has subsided and come back out cautiously. "Happy hour" is at dusk. That's the time to cast on the lady of the P.M. for her newly adopted sons and daughters. Within minutes you'll be victorious.

River People

The evolution of a river is a complex process shaped by events that occur with the changing balance of natural interaction. Humans perhaps play the most important role in determining a river's destiny. The Pere Marquette draws people almost in a spiritual, mystical way. A river is shaped by personalities and vice versa. The interaction of the two can set the stage for a river dynasty or its ultimate decimation. It is a constant saga of different people with attitudes, creative skills, political astuteness, enthusiasm and sometimes shortsightedness that allows the "band to play on." Yet river people are first and foremost fisher men and women. What happens to them later impacts the future course a river will follow.

Zimmy Nolph at his fly tying bench.

◆

Zimmy Nolph, now 87, was one of the first guides on the Pere Marquette, teaming up with Fred Sedlecki of Ed's Sport Shop and Herman Stephanson to guide the river. Born in Reynoldsburg, Pennsylvania, he fished as a boy in the mountains for brook trout with green cord line wrapped to a birch sapling. Well-digging took him to Michigan. "When I saw this here Pere Marquette River, I said, this was for me." He became a guide in the summer, catering to wealthy corporate outings by Ford, Chrysler and other well-to-do executives from all over the Midwest. He experienced a magnificent trout fishery with healthy fighting steelhead. Today he blames the river's problems on the introduction of the Pacific salmon which "shift the streambeds, banks and gravel areas around like kids in a sandbox" after they come through to spawn. "If God would have meant for such large things to be in a small place like this, they'd be here." says Zimmy. He blames a possible downfall of the trout fishery and insect populations to the treatment of TFM (3-trifluoromethyl-4-nitrophenol) lamperycide every four years. "There is no hope left for her." (the P.M.) he laments.

Bob Nicholson, longtime river guide, owner of the Baldwin Creek Motel, president of the Pere Marquette Watershed Council and an ardent conservation activist, knows the P.M. very well—he is the modern day dean of the river. His charming and gregarious personality, combined with interesting storytelling amuse his very dedicated clients. It is a pleasure to watch Bob fish his team of traditional wet flies and fool wise native brown trout. Bob describes the people that visit the P.M.: "In my role as a fishing guide I see a lot of people. Most of them I categorize as users and takers. They use the resource, take everything they can from it, and go home and forget about it—that encompasses 95 percent. The other five percent express an interest in the resource and will give their energy or their dollars to preserve it—that five percent keeps this river alive and well".

Jim and Tom Johnson who own and operate Johnson's Pere Marquette Lodge, represent the new age of river people. Hailing from Ohio, they've fished the P.M. since their early teenage years, prior to establishing their beautiful cedar lodge, guide service and fly shop. Jim comments that he was inspired to pursue the P.M. by Ernie Schwiebert's writings of the river and his "Deer Lick" steelhead article. "I feel like I barely scratched the surface of this river in the last 10 years." he comments due to the river's vast unexplored territory. Talking to Jim you sense a great deal of enthusiasm and optimism about what the future holds for the Pere Marquette. "The people you run into on this river are in a different class from other anglers. Even when it's crowded, people are courteous and friendly." Jim is an excellent fly fisherman, entrepreneur and overall visionary when it comes to the ecological and fishery needs that the P.M. will require to remain a world class river. He appreciates and respects the multi-dimensionalism that the river offers with salmon, steelhead and brown trout—he runs their fly shop to encompass the entire gamut of these experiences.

Tom Johnson is a thinking man's fly fisherman. Very introspective, curious and always analytical, he could be the G.E.M. Skues of the Pere Marquette. It is very enlightening to talk with Tom about the various hatches, anadromous fish behavior and any scientific light that can be infused into the fly fishing dynamics of the river.

◆

Guide Bob Nicholson points Laurie Supinski to a rising trout.

Laurie Supinski casts below Lower Branch Bridge.

Dick Pobst, owner and operator of the Orvis Thornapple Shop in Ada, is a master entomological fly fisher. His book *Trout Stream Insects* has helped all in the sport have a better grip on the P.M. and its hatch complexity. It is a pleasure to sit and chat with him about his passion for the gray drake which is the primary hatch on the river.

Walt Grau and John Kluesing are the river's ultimate fish tracking and catching guides. If there is a brown trout swimming in the Florida Keys, these two gentlemen will find it and catch it on a dry fly. Walt is an innovative guide, expert fly tier and technique specialist who recently is promoting Spey rod and sink-tip line fishing as opposed to "drift fishing or chuck-and-duck methods." John Kluesing spends his summers in Maine as an instructor for the L.L. Bean Fly Fishing School. It's gratifying to drift with these gentlemen who are always upbeat and fun even when the action gets tense and heated up. They have the eyes of a hawk and are ever so mindful of their client's needs.

The Pere Marquette draws thousands of people each year to its waters. It has survived the ravages of the loggers, the onslaught of the Pacific salmon invasion and the heated-up angling pressure that it currently receives. Yet the river flourishes and prospers from year to year, providing experiences for all that visit and fish it. The P.M. has hundreds of supporters who are both close and far and united by organizations like the Pere Marquette

Watershed Council, Trout Unlimited and The Federation of Fly Fishermen.

The Pere Marquette has a lot of friends—though it needs more! The river wants to be everything to everyone—she's ever so empathetic. Greed, personal gain and shortsightedness will destroy her. "Everything in nature needs a rest." Zimmy Nolph told me. Maybe this old lady could use one once in awhile. Come and enjoy. But be ever so gentle and thoughtful. Let the mystique of this special river capture and entice you to become a river person for life.

Guide Services, Resources, Places of Interest, Restaurants and Lodging

Baldwin Creek Motel—Rte. 3, Box 3282, Baldwin, Michigan 49304 (616) 745-4401.

Owner and guide Bob Nicholson has an excellent knowledge of the Pere Marquette along with jet sled guide service on the Muskegon and Manistee Rivers, Michigan's premier tailwater trout and salmon fisheries. His wife Christa keeps the rooms immaculate and affordable.

Early morning October steam as angler waits for Chinook salmon at Maple Leaf.

Johnson's Pere Marquette Lodge—An Orvis-endorsed Outfitter—South M-37, Rte. 1, Box 1290, Baldwin, Michigan 49304 (616) 745-3972.

The ultimate fly fisher's destination for the Pere Marquette. Jim and Tom Johnson, both excellent fly fishermen, run one of the best fly shops in the state. Locally tied flies, excellent guides, stream information and a warm welcome awaits you. A beautiful cedar lodge (and streamside cabins) reminiscent of a well done Alaskan lodge with fireplace, living room, fly tying area and rooms equipped with kitchen areas, Jacuzzi's and an overall spirit of the Michigan outdoors. Guide service available on "The Circle" of rivers adjacent to the P.M.—Little Manistee, Big Manistee, Sable, Muskegon, White etc.

Ed's Sport Shop—712 Michigan Avenue (on M-37), P.O. Box 487, Baldwin, Michigan 49304 (616) 745-4974.

Doug and Loretta Loomis run a fine sport shop with an excellent selection of fly tackle and flies. Friendly and helpful service and accurate stream information are always available.

Thornapple Orvis Shop—Thornapple Village, Box 133, Ada, Michigan (616) 676-0177.

---◆---

A spring steelhead float.

Dick Pobst is one of the most knowledgeable entomological fly fishermen. His shop looks like a New England boutique. Nancy Pobst creates a delightful setting.

Barothy Lodge—P.O. Box 7478 Barothy Road, Walhalla, Michigan 49458 (616) 898-2340.

Right in the heart of *Hex* country on the P.M., this excellent lodge offers great river access and a year-round retreat. Swimming, tennis, cross country ski trails.

Streamside—An Orvis Shop—Grand Traverse Resort, Boulevard E-4, Williamsburg, Michigan 49690 (616) 938-5338.

No trip to P.M. country would be complete without a trip to artsy Traverse City and the Grand Traverse Resort, home of one of the world's top golf courses. The shop has an Abercrombie and Fitch atmosphere, knowledgeable service and friendly and inviting staff.

Michigan Department of Natural Resources—District 6, Cadillac, Michigan (616) 775-9727.

Leo Mrozinski, District Biologist is the expert on the Pere Marquette. His advice and knowledge is extensive.

Huron—Manistee National Forest—Cadillac, Michigan (616) 775-2421. Information on guide licenses, camping etc.

DNR Fishing Hotline—(517) 373-0908.
Up-to-date fishing reports by region.

Michigan Travel Bureau—P.O. Box 3393, Livonia, Michigan 48151-3393 or call 800-5432 YES.

Restaurants

Emerson Lake Inn—7786 E. U.S. 10, Walhalla, Michigan (616) 757-2385.

Excellent service and food—Perhaps the best in Mason County. House specialties include prime rib and seafood—great salad bar.

Sporties Bar—Downtown Baldwin on M-37 (616) 745-3932.

Fun late night spot—river guide hangout at pool table—excellent half pound sportie burgers. Serves until 1:30 a.m.

Skii's—M-37 North of Baldwin (616) 745-3200.
Fresh walleye is the house specialty.

Edie's Log Bar—Downtown Baldwin (616) 745-4421.
Good pub food with late night serving.

Big Star Lake Inn—Star Lake Road, Baldwin, Michigan (616) 898-2993.
Prime rib is the specialty.

All Seasons—M-37 Baldwin (616) 745-7731.
A cozy country diner with great broasted chicken.

Main Stream Cafe—M-37, Baldwin, Michigan (616) 745-3377.
French dip is the house specialty.